THE CIRCUS

Media, Politics, & Power
In the Era of Donald Trump

LYNN MORRIS

Library of Congress Cataloguing-in-Publication Data

Morris, Lynn

The Circus: Media, Politics, & Power

in the Era of Donald Trump

Library of Congress Control Number: 2020911097

ISBN:9798654239013

DEDICATION

For my husband

CONTENTS

ACKNOWLEDGMENTS

My study of media, politics and power has spanned nearly 30 years. I would like to thank three legends of communications theory who helped me along the way, specifically my professors at The University of South Carolina in Columbia: retired professor emeritus Lowndes F. Stephens; the late Robert Jones, who was instrumental in the establishment of the Minnesota Poll; and Kent Sidel. Though I cannot speak to whether they would concur with the political notions expressed in this book, I am grateful to have had the opportunity to learn the basics of communications research from them.

A special thank you to all those who participated in my initial study, specifically foreign bureau chiefs at The New York Times, the Washington Post, and elsewhere, who gave generously of their time to discuss the interplay of reporter preparedness and stereotyping in the public discourse.

Journalism is ultimately an exercise in speaking truth to power. The current era indicates the continuing relevance of good reporting and the ongoing need for an informed electorate to maintain a free society.

PROLOGUE—STEP RIGHT UP

Travelling circuses were a main source of entertainment in the early part of the 20th century. Travelling caravans would come into town, set up shop, and bilk the locals out of their money in short order.

The ringmaster, who controlled the proceedings of the three ring circus, was a combination of showman and all-out huckster. He hyped the crowd. He managed the acts. He was responsible for everything from the flying trapeze to the man-eating tigers.
Donald J. Trump, the 45th President of the United States, is perhaps the most dazzling ringmaster in all of history. And his mind-boggling three ring circus of confusion, intolerance, and all-out avarice, would give the greatest huckster of the last century a run for their money.

It's as if he's got the entire world balancing a rubber ball on the end of their nose like a well trained, yet very nervous, seal.

I am writing this from self-imposed COVID-19 on my farm in the mountains of western North Carolina. More than 100,000 people in the United States have died of the virus.

The elephants, it seems, are stampeding from the circus tent and there's not a damn thing any of us can do.

The killing of an unarmed black man, George Floyd in Minneapolis, has set the entire country into a morass of rioting.

To Donald Trump, like any good ringmaster, doesn't see this as a problem. The less you believe him, the greater the challenge becomes. He goes on air every day and lies to your face. And even though you'd like to believe, you know in your heart it's all a bunch of smoke and mirrors.

Reporters protest with all the effectiveness of a petulant child, whining about their treatment, bickering with the Bully in Chief from his Bully pulpit, staring in utter amazement as he relentlessly badgers them, turns on his well-polished heel and waltzes his fat ass back inside the portico doors.

The public, meanwhile, sits frightened in their homes, hoarding food, worrying about their bills, fretting over their children, hoping that the man-eating tigers of the pandemic don't come to their doors. "I feel," said a friend, "that I am only sitting here waiting to die." Another, a 95 year old woman, said, "I feel like I'm a prison."

This is a hell for people who are alone, who are lonely, who will soon in any case meet death, most likely alone in a hospital or, worse yet, via videochat.

Trump is not idle as the tigers escape from their cages, the elephants run amok, and the circus tent goes up in flames. In fact, he casually waltzes off to one of his golf courses. His son-in-law and know-nothing advisor Jared Kushner heads to the conference room to make more deals with the Israelis. Stephen Miller, an evil little toad and architect of doom, heads to some evil little bunker to devise other ways to antagonize minorities and strip thousands of souls of their civil liberties.

If you're looking for a culprit, there's a lot of blame to go around. Trump is a master of blame, calling out Democratic governors, the World Health Organization, the United Nations, the Chinese, Anthony Fauci, CNN, Twitter, Mark Zuckerburg, everyone from the Pope to Rosie MacDonald for the decline of the economy, the medical carnage, a failing infrastructure as appealing as day old circus popcorn.

We sit in our rooms, binge-watching baking shows on the BBC, fashioning masks for health workers whose work has become the philanthropic project du jour for so many women with sewing skills who want to do something, anything, to protect the people they love in their communities.

Remember that old bumper sticker adage about the 'bake sale to buy a bomb?'

Who knew that we would live to see a day when that plays out in real time, when women are sewing up cotton masks in their suburban craft rooms while the Liar in Chief heads to Mar-a-Lago for another round of dishonest golf?

If you're living in this world, you feel it. Is there anyone who wakes up with anything less than fear and loathing of the days ahead? How did we get in this hall of mirrors? And how will we survive in one piece?

To Democrats, the need to get Trump out of his cushy chair in the Oval Office and on to federal prison where he no doubt belongs, is usurped only the inexplicable, unfathomable, unmanageable need to win and win big in the November election.
To armchair cowboys and media pundits, the trouble with Trump is Trump himself.

And, like a scruffy, frat boy boyfriend your freshman daughter brings home for Thanksgiving dinner, his ascent to power and dizzying grip on a portion of the electorate is baffling. How did he get here? And, politely, how can we show him the door? Or, put more succinctly, how can we get Trump out of office without seeing the whole country going up in flames?

Why do so many people fall for Trump's shameless charade? And how is he accumulating more power while a portion of the country, possibly that small but influential portion that defeated him in the popular vote against Hillary Clinton in 2016 and sat in stunned silence when he captured the electoral college and walked with his stiletto-heeled, nude model third wife into the White House, stands by with white bread liberal incredulity?

As a graduate student at The University of South Carolina's College of Journalism and Mass Communications, I designed one of the first studies that examined the role that media preparedness plays in the public discourse and stereotyping in international politics, specifically stereotyping of the former Soviet Union and how that stereotyping in the US media affected the development and implementation of US foreign policy.

I interviewed the foreign bureau chiefs of major new outlets such as **The New York Times, Washington Post, the Los Angeles Times,** and the directors of political think tanks such as the Brookings Institute, the New York University Center for War, Peace, and the News Media, and the Carter Center for Peace at Emory University. The purpose of these conversations was to ask the experts what they felt were the important components that any reporters presenting news should understand about a culture.

Does reporter education affect accuracy and effectiveness of their reporting. How could we make reporters better? And would the improvement of basic knowledge about a country improve not only the public discourse but contain the explosive stereotyping that has devastating effects on our economy, our rule of law, international relations and the way forward.

I pinpointed four basic components of society that contribute to the public's understanding of the issues—politics, history, geography and culture. I then designed a multiple choice survey research instrument to better understand the basic knowledge that beginning reporters bring to their craft.

I have spoken about the interplay of media, politics and power at meetings including the United Nations in New York, the Gendering Asia Conference at Copenhagen University in Denmark, and sat on a panel at the Women & Politics in Asia Forum in Islamabad, Pakistan. Understanding stereotyping is key to understanding the otherwise baffling ascent of Donald Trump to the White House.

First, Trump employs a very specific arsenal of political speech and stereotyping strategies, both verbal and nonverbal, to coalesce his base and solidify his power.

Secondly, the manner in which reporters do their work and their own, personal understanding of the United States in the four mentioned sectors (politics, history, geography and culture) is critical to Donald Trump's ability to consolidate political power around a few stereotypical ideas.

His daily interaction with the media and the resulting stories, far from being random, plays into his conceptualization of that power. It is not random. Though it appears extremely antagonistic on the surface of things, the confrontations in the White House Press Room actually serve to enhance his grip on his power and solidify his base behind a few simple ideas that are reinforced in a very systematic manner.

He is very much in control of the narrative as reporters grapple not only with the challenges of doing their work in a very antagonistic environment (which is not really a big deal, as the relationship between reporters and their subjects is by its very definition antagonistic). Where the media are failing has more to do with their own lack of knowledge about the United States within the sectors and their subsequent inability to frame stories that use context to counteract misinformation and stereotypical speech from the top.

The 24 hour news cycle, vertical integration and news on demand, the rise of social media platforms such as Twitter and Facebook have all contributed to the dereliction of not only media sources but public literacy of the issues and their relevance not only in real time but their place in history. In 2002, the National Geographic Roper Geographic Literacy Study found that most US students could not identify the Pacific Ocean on a map; the land mass of the Pacific Ocean covers 50% of the globe.

An ill-informed,   racist, Republican base plays well into Trump's concepts of isolationism and nationalism.

Context in reporting takes time and effort. Without it, consumers are doomed to 5 minute sound bytes and screaming pundits who only deliver their views without any sense of the long view in which we all must live.

For his part, Trump is a shameless opportunist, a carnival barker huckster who runs the government like a third rate reality show and makes his decisions solely on emotion, eschewing the experts.

Far from being scandalized by such behavior, his base is energized by the ignorance as it is familiar to them: it echoes their own preference for emotion and sensationalism over the far less sexy strategy of facts. It fuels their hate. It fuels their desire for control. It fuels their false sense of superiority. It allows them to skate over the thin ice of context and yet, somehow, miraculously, pull each other to the other side. It is less complicated, less messy, less deep that actually seeking deep knowledge. It is the knee jerk reaction to a question that in reality requires the exactitude of a brain surgeon.

Trump gets away with this because it feels good to the people it energizes; they don't know and they don't want to know.

I've never liked the phrase 'perfect storm.' It in no way encapsulates what happens in real time, the implication that perfect things come together to create unique conditions and that those conditions are in some way unique to all of history.

America in 2020 is getting what it deserves. The dignified opposition only holds itself by sheer resolve; by choosing love over hate, wisdom over ignorance, our higher selves over our basest instincts.

Despite all that, the tigers roam the street, threatening to undo us. Civilization is a thinly veiled attempt to keep that wildness, that base instinct, the rough and awful edges of humanity from spilling over into real life. Can we walk our way back from the edge? Can we cultivate a civil society that is truly civil, based on wise decisions and an informed electorate, inoculated from hearsay and stereotyping and power plays that threaten to undo us?

Isn't it time we abandon the Facebookian hucksterism, the isolationism that threatens to undo us. Spawned during Reagan's senseless Evil Empire rhetoric, the world is deserving of so much more. We deserve reporters who do their jobs and do them well, not falling prey to the bullying tactics of sycophants and their enablers.

I once met Jesse Jackson and his security detail in an elevator at the Hyatt Hotel in Greenville, South Carolina. I saw him previously at the check-in desk but was still rather surprised when he got on the elevator with me. "You scared me," I said, almost involuntarily, and he laughed. I meant startled, not scared, but this Freudian slip perhaps said more about my Southern upbringing and concepts of what it means to be on an elevator with a man of another race than I would like. Later, I read in an interview that he had famously said, "The only thing to fear is the fear right here."

We are living in a time of fear. Nonetheless, we have access to more information, more possibilities for getting it right, more connection than ever before. How do we understand Trump's well-crafted use of stereotyping to control our behavior? How do we hold the media accountable for their reporting and the journalistic frames that influence us? And, perhaps more importantly, how do we use the tools before us to make good decisions our rights and responsibilities and the road ahead.

The tigers are loose. The elephants are running amok in the street. The ringmaster, Donald Trump, is derisively smirking at us from the center ring.

Only we can decide if we can cultivate a society and a demeanor that allows us to get home in one piece.

CHAPTER 1—HE HATE ME

In the late 1980s, the short-lived XFL took professional football by a very short lived storm. Billed as rougher and sexier than that bastion of American beer drinking-- the NFL--the XFL was filled with colorful characters, perhaps none of whom was more colorful than running back Rod Smart, known on the field as "He Hate Me."

In a promo for the league, the affable Smart holds up his jersey and proclaims something to effect that his opponents hated him because he was faster, stronger, and, well, smarter than the average player. It was a hell of a moniker to have on the back of a football jersey, sort of like those cartoon bubbles that hover over the heads of comic strip characters, telling you what the person is thinking inside. I'm (fill in the blank with your own superlative) and hence he hate me.

It was a cultural marker filled with both swagger and despair, the use of a vernacular that was at once charming and disturbing to those outside of the African-American community who would instantly think, at first, that Hate is missing an 's' and then wonder at the bombast of the word hate on the football field (which is perhaps one of the few places where the word actually belongs).

Language is power. It's a tool to organize the world, convey meaning, develop communities and, yes, to tear things apart.
Trump is a master manipulator. And despite his image in the minds of the left as a blundering buffoon, stumbling over words, mispronouncing, full of bombast and swagger, his intent is far more sinister and calculating that it appears.

Communications researchers give a lot of thought to the ways in which humans construct meaning. When we name something, be it Shakespeare or Snoop Dogg, we are sending a signal, a code, to the person on the other end. "See, I'm calling this thing by this name, don't you agree?"

Trump is no Churchill nor even a Ronald Reagan. He's in a class all by himself when it comes to malapropism. His extemporaneous speech is often baffling. There is one aspect of rhetorical and persuasive language in which he almost reigns supreme in modern times.

Long before he became president, he perfected the art of the epithet, a short catchphrase that works as shorthand to depict (and usually stereotype) another person. .

Trump's outrageous epithets stun his opponents and send an immediate, electric charge to his followers. Yes, they think enthusiastically, that's right! That's exactly the way we see it! And every time he hurls at epithet at one of his rivals, his ingroup feels more powerful, stronger, more entitled, and on the right side by siding with him.

The epithet is a linguistic trick as old as the ancient theater of Greece.

In ancient Greece, poetry and theatre held the culture together. It was the outlet for political commentary. Social development depended upon the sharing of common experiences (much like today, though, of course there was no electricity nor Internet). Theatre was all important in this and the stories told were sung, as in poetry, and featured characters and themes that were instantly familiar to the audience and relevant to the culture.

Because these stories were serialized, appearing over multiple evenings or even lasting for years (think installments of a TV series or a video game here for some modern context), the playwright needed a way to characterize the heroes in such a way that they were instantly recognizable to the audience without building up a lot of backstory. To achieve this characterization, the writer had to do two things—first, establish the traits that he wanted to highlight and secondly, explain them in a kind of shorthand so that the audience would know immediately who was appearing and how that would be important to the drama that would lie ahead.

A chorus stood on either side of an arch-like stage—good on one side, evil on the other, god in the middle. These choruses would move the action along by singing poetry back and forth (this is known as strophe and antistrophe, but one easy way to remember is it's like those Bugs Bunny cartoons where an angel sits on one shoulder and the devil on the other.

Choruses in the ancient Greek theater thus relied heavily on the use to language to characterize or stereotype the characters who might appear. This is done via the use of epithets, a kind of shorthand that explains the character consistently so that the audience can instantly recognize who was about to appear and, more importantly, what that person was like in the context of the play or the relevance of the culture.

Hence, "bright eyed Athena" or "Brave Odysseus" or "Loyal Penelope."
Epithets are a kind of shorthand familiar to the listeners. In ancient Greece, when the descriptive term for the Greek gods or the Greek heroes were sung to the audience, they would sigh in unison. They knew what was going to happen next in much the same way that your favorite musician launches into the chords of a familiar refrain.

Sound familiar?

Think "Lying Hillary," "Sleepy Joe Biden," or "Pocahontas."

Epithets are instrumental in what communications researchers call code-sharing. It's a kind of verbal shorthand, a way that groups use to construct meaning. It's a skill that starts at birth, one way that we all use to identify our role within groups and the fast track to our relationships.

When we code share, we establish an in-group, a culture of familiarity that we slowly populate with other concepts and ideas upon which we agree. It might be a positive thing (calling your spouse "sweetie" would be one example, a term of endearment that changes and adapts as your relationship changes and adapts) or it might take the darker cloak of hate speech.

Epithets are a powerful tool in the arsenal of bullies and garden variety haters. They allow the 'ingroup' to feel positive about their agreement (even if it might be a negative thing, a person who uses a pejorative for a racial or social group is not trying to be positive, he's trying to influence those around him to think in the way that he thinks).

Code sharing thus strengthens one group (the "believers" or those in agreement) at the detriment of the people being described. Further, the distance between the familiar (the 'in-group') and the different ('the outgroup') is exaggerated. Anyone who has ever been called a name by an 8th grade bully knows that epithets pack a powerful punch to the outgroup.

Stereotyping via epithets and other linguistic code-sharing devices is one of the favored methods employed by Trump via his school-yard bullying of his political rivals. Hence, people who disagree are 'snowflakes.' Recently, in a social media debate, a Trumper told me to 'take a cookie on my way out.'

The level of childish snark seems to be at an all-time high. Trump is a ringmaster when using the fears and superstitions of his base to help them feel better about themselves. He forcefully supported the Birther movement and used it to continuously disparage Barack Obama.

Right wing pundits (and general nut job conspiracy theorists) such as Rush Limbaugh and Sean Hannity repeatedly refer to Obama as "Hussein" (his middle name) in an effort to draw into question his allegiance to the United States, his legitimacy as a political candidate.

As a bonus, Trump was able to rile up the prejudices of his political base, harkening back to the first Iraq War, 9/11, and a Pandora's box of conspiracy theories relating to everyone from Bill Clinton to Osama Bin Laden. The mental shorthand, the free association code share, was clear. Hussain as in Saddam Hussain. A foreigner. Non-white. And, hence, to the uneducated portion of Trump's base, possibly un-American.

His media flunkies such as Limbaugh and Hannity willingly do his bidding, his political base gets energized by the conversation and throw another log on the fire with their own, ill-crafted, amateurish sleuthing and discussions of the 'deep state on social media.

The stakes in geopolitics are much higher than those faced by an 9th grade bully. The extrinsic rewards is that the in-group, who create meaning for themselves and stereotype the other out of bounds of actually reality. This allows the ingroup to feel stronger and more empowered at the expense of the 'weaker' party.

After all, how do you counter the argument when someone in a position of authority calls you Pocahontas. Do you respond by proving your Native American heritage? Do you try to invigorate a less powerful minority group that has been traditionally sidelined, a group with few political resources and no seat at the table to begin with?

Talk is cheap. If you've ever been on the wrong side of bullying, there at the 8th grade lunch table (where this type of 'rhetoric,' actually it is shameful to even call it that, much less to discover that a sitting United States president indulges in it), you know that there is nothing—NOTHING—you can say or do or be that thwarts the death spiral of stereotyping once it starts. There is nothing you can do to tamp down the power of this tactic, to diffuse the feeling of superiority that it gives to the in group that buys into the notion of their superiority, to make it go away. It is the same feeling that makes bullied people jump off bridges and eschew their high school reunions.

The Democrats seem to think that a sense of righteous indignation will get Trump to stop, to work as a conciliator and 'bring the country together.'

And yet, thinking back to your experiences in junior high school (where this 'tactic' has its origins), did the expression of outrage ever make a bully hang up the bullying? Did you ever see that pimply, pushy boy from school, the one who laughed and you and got him minions to join in the torment, suddenly say, "Oh, you are right, Bubba, you are not a dork. Your name is James. Have a seat. Have some ice cream?" Then why do we expect the Bully in Chief and his nude model wife to suddenly come to their senses and remove the political epithets from their lexicon of dirty tricks?

It didn't happen in junior high and it's not gonna happen now. The sooner that the Democrats realize that one way they are being had is with this clever trick of language, the easiest way that Trump is solidifying his base at the expense of the reasonable voters on the other side, the sooner they will be able to form a strategy that will bring down the Bully in Chief and possibly allow them to win the election in November, 2020.

Once epithets take hold in the public conversation (both good and bad), they are impossible to remove with reason. You cannot shout louder than a bully. You cannot one up them, no matter how you try. What you can do is stop responding. This is harder than it seems. But how would Elizabeth Warren's future have been different if, rather than spending an ounce of energy attempting to prove her Native American heritage or being outraged at Trump's rhetoric, she had instead redirected the conversation to an issue that actually mattered, say, the economy?

Part of Trump's power lies in this supreme power of distraction. This is the hallmark of any great ringmaster, the ability to distract.

It is almost as if you cannot believe what you are seeing, that he would mock a reporter with a disability, or call a woman fat or hysterical, or gloat about his romantic conquests or say that he would probably be dating his daughter if she wasn't his daughter. When you express your disbelief, just in the same way you expressed your shock and embarrassment when that 8th grade bully tied your shoes to the book rack under your desk, you are playing into the reinforcement of those ideas to his base. They might be unseemly (they are). They might be ridiculous (they are). They definitely are beneath you. But every time you respond, every time you express your outrage, they get stronger and you get weaker. And this, my friends, is not the way to win in November. It's the way to make certain that those monikers will linger around forever. The more you talk about them, the stronger they get.

Let us consider for a moment the recent efforts of First Lady of the United States, the former nude model Melania Trump. Her 'pet project' as First Lady is apparently anti-bullying, with the somewhat baffling and utterly nonsensical slogan extolling America's school children to "Be Best."

The stiletto-clad Melania, apparently reformed from her days of lounging on rented private jets wearing nothing but a sloe-eyed glance and a few jewels, says that the Be Best campaign has some positive goals:

"By promoting values such as healthy living, encouragement, kindness, and respect, parents, teachers, and other adults can help prepare children for their futures. With those values as a solid foundation, children will be able to better deal with the evils of the opioid crisis and avoid negative social media interaction."

This from a woman who visited a McAllen, Texas INS detention center for children in 2016 clad in a cryptic, $39 Zara jacket with the slogan, "I really don't care, do U?" emblazoned on her back. If you really do care, you need to show it by not responding to those who apparently parade around not caring.

The Democrats must reframe the narrative around their own ideals if they are to win in November. This means not responding to Trumps' epithets and ignoring the First Lady's graphic fashion choices. It means understanding that language, all language, is power and stereotypical to some degree. Trump lost the popular vote in 2016 by 2%. He did not win by a landslide. He eeked out the electoral college vote to capture the White House much in the way that 8th grade bully (shall we give him a name? Shall we call him Ronald Dumph?) grabbed the chocolate chip cookie off your lunch tray while you were untying your shoes from underneath the table and wouldn't give it back to you. By focusing on his language instead of his ideas, the Democrats undermine their own authority to the benefit of the incumbent.

Trump loves to refer to himself as a "wartime President" (it's a war that he has created, a war of his own devising, but, to quote George W. Bush, "Facts are stupid things"). He also loves to harken to that great Republican Abraham Lincoln. My theory in this is that Lincoln is just far back enough for Trump to feel safe that no one really remembers what he was about.

Lincoln once wrote a letter to his son Willie's teacher about bullying. In this letter, he noted that a "bully is the easiest to lick." This might not be a true story. What is true is that bullying, and the bullying language of the epithet, energizes like minded people and leaves outliers on the other side. This is known as the ingroup/outgroup phenomenon.

It is key to understanding stereotyping and why minorities, women, people of color, immigrants, the media, and others who somehow acquire the President's seemingly endless ire, are at a tremendous disadvantage when shaping the narrative that is so crucial to the 2020 election.

The best approach is to reframe by ignoring the pejorative language and, as Michele Obama would put it, "go high when they go low."

Remember, they really don't care.

We do.

CHAPTER 2—THE IN CROWD

On the first day of June, 2020, President Donald J. Trump made a speech in the White House Rose garden. The weekend, usually reserved for college graduations, early summer weddings, and garden parties, had been one of tremendous strife and violence in America.

On May 25th, 2020, an unarmed black man, George Floyd, was killed by a white Minneapolis, Minnesota police officer, Derek Chauvin, who kept his knee on the right side of Floyd's neck for 8 minutes and 45 seconds while the handcuffed Floyd, who had been arrested for attempting to pass a counterfeit $20 bill at a small grocery store, pleaded for his life. Three other police offices, Tou Thao, J. Alexander Kueng, and Thomas K Lane participated in Floyd's arrest and failed to render aid as he begged, saying "I can't breathe."

The killing of George Floyd sparked a tinderbox of riots, looting, public protest (both peaceful and violent), the involvement and destabilizing element of hate groups such as the Aryan Nation, the

Ku Klux Klan, and ANTIFA. It was a situation made demonstrably worse by Trump's unwillingness to denounce the violence, choosing instead to hide in a bunker under the White House while the District of Columbia went up in flames.

It was as if 400 years of oppression and missed opportunity came to a horrible, festering head on that cool June evening. The devastating COVID-19 virus had killed more than 100,000 people in the United States alone, while Trump prevaricated, looking desperately for a political rival upon which to pin the blame. As crowds collected outside the White House, standing peacefully but speaking truth to power and expecting a leader, the President who had so unwittingly proclaimed himself a wartime president, had to eventually step out of his cushy underground lair with a gaggle of pasty white advisors and his ever-president, plasticine daughter Ivanka and son-in-law Jared Kushner and do something.

It was the perfect time to make a statement. And he did make a statement, a silent one of sorts, but it was hardly presidential. And it was nothing if not opaque.

Instead of offering hope to a country that was rapidly falling into what seemed to pundits all over the world as a death spiral of the COVID-19 virus, record unemployment, erratic leadership and now civil unrest and racial violence, Trump chose to proclaim himself the "President of Law and Order" and hint at nefarious solutions including a heavy military presence and martial law. He then employed the National Guard to fire tear gas and fire rubber bullets on the protestors gathered in front of the White House to clear the path for his lily white contingent to cross the street to St. John's Episcopal Church, where he stood on the steps of that boarded-up landmark, a landmark he called the 'church of presidents' although he had only visited once during the week of his inauguration.

There, having dispersed the crowd, Trump stood on the steps of the church holding a black leather Bible, His base, the in-crowd, cheered via Fox News at what they saw as an unapologetic stance of religious solidarity. He is, according to some, the "president chosen by God." The Democrats and other liberals, the 'out group,' were enraged.

Many elements of this situation are as opaque as that tear gas sprayed into the eyes of the peaceful crowd in LaFayette Square. We cannot see our way clear. We wonder if the United States of America will survive.

Trump stood in front of the boarded-up church, his arms out in front of him, restless with his ill-fitting suit covering his pot belly and his far-too-long tie making a dubious sartorial statement, his eyes small and threatening, his comb-over glistening in the late afternoon sun of the nation's capital like that pale yellow synthetic hair that used to adore the rubber head of Malibu Barbie. He seemed tentative, nervous, less of a leader than a figurehead or, at the very least, a person who was attempting to use all of the cultural and visual markers at his disposal to send a message to his 'base,' his core group of Trumpers and Trumpettes and die-hard believers who feel that his leadership is nothing short of heaven-sent.

The pundits on right-wing, conservative radio seized upon the moment. Fox News, in all of their Trump-adoring zeal, were elated. The Bishop in whose archdiocese the church belongs, was a little less thrilled. "I was outraged that he felt that he had the license to do that, and that he would abuse our sacred symbols and our sacred space in that way," she said.

She shouldn't have been surprised. At the heart of this situation, the meteoric rise of Donald Trump and the almost tornadic environment of disease, unemployment, international disdain, racial inequity, and civil rest has more do to with our understanding of power and its symbolism than it does with actual, working political strategies that might pull the country out of the abyss.

Through the tear gas, one thing was made clear.

We are being had.

Harkening perhaps back to Alexander Graham Bell and that adage we learned about the invention of the telephone, "Mr. Watson, I need you!"—the public tends to think of the media as a strictly linear exchange. You have something you want to say, you say it, and a recipient picks it up as easily as a catcher catches a ball while playing a game on a summer afternoon.

In reality, communication is nothing like that. It is full of nuance. Rife with the possibility of being both understood and misunderstood. There are countless, intervening variables that come into play, many of them hidden from all of the parties involved, including the people on both sides. If you've ever played that childhood game, telephone, you know that a message at the start is rarely the same message at the end.

The symbols deployed in front of the White House on June 1st, 2020 were never intended to bring the country together. And those who feel that one of the chief objectives of the current commander in chief is to bring people together, command the military, work on both sides of the aisle, address our interests throughout the world, and make the country a better place in which to live haven't been paying attention for the past three years.

Donald Trump's goal is not to bring people together. His goal is to use all of the tricks in his bag to reinforce the power that he already has—the voters, the companies, the personal alliances, the international governments that will pay him lip service. He doesn't have to create messages that propel the United States of America as a country forward; he only has to create messages and organize symbols that energize his base, thus creating an environment that will allow him to maintain his current position for another four years or more, depending on the legal circumstances he can craft for himself and his cronies in the meantime.

Recently, Ivanka Trump, daughter in chief, was asked by Robin Roberts on ABCNews if the "lock her up" slogan the Republicans so handily applied to Hillary Clinton would serve the same purpose for Ivanka's own errant emails. "No, it doesn't," she replied, whimsically, a coquettish response more suited to a question about the shoes you're planning to wear to the prom than a question about the potential felony of using a personal email account for public business.

The organization of social groups is a complex interaction for humans. It involves verbal cues, non-verbal cues, social contracts, aspirations, and something known as 'code sharing,' in which participants in an 'exchange' of communication use a kind of verbal, non-verbal, and physical shorthand to create identity within a group. Code-sharing leads us to something know as 'convex perception' or 'the ingroup/outgroup phenomenon.' Understanding this is key to understanding Trump's well crafted strategy of language and manipulation, a strategy that infuriates the outsiders while speaking only to his base. It is not the strategy of a leader who wants to bring people together. It is a strategy used by tyrants to enhance their power at the expense of others. And it is a strategy that is tailor made for a time where people get their news in sound bytes at the expense of the written word.

All across America, people sat in stunned silence in 2016 as Trump lost the popular vote by 2% and yet managed to secure the electoral college vote and thus the election. Among his base, Trump seemed like the ultimate disrupter—irreverent yet familiar from his days as the focal point of 'Celebrity Apprentice' and it's memorable catchphrase, "you're fired!" To people who were suffering economically, Trump seemed like a person who had lived out the American Dream of the average white person in middle America—wealthy, being chauffeured through the streets of New York in a brand new Cadillac sedan emblazoned with his initials. He had a lot of the codes that most men of his demographic would want for themselves, if they were being honest. He had a sexy wife. He owned casinos, apartment buildings, universities, television properties, swanky golf clubs around the world, a private jet, a steak company, a winery. He was, as humorist Fran Leibowitz once quipped, "A poor person's idea of a rich person."

If you look at elections in terms of code-sharing, it's easy to see how Obama beat Republican challengers John McCain and Sarah Palin and paved his way to the White House. For all his heroism, McCain harkened back to a time in history that many Americans barely knew and, if they did know, they wanted to forget. His straight-talking rhetoric often seemed unbalanced and anachronistic. All that, coupled with the Alaskan wilderness vibe (and subsequent, rhetorical fumbling) of Sarah Palin, who perhaps appealed with white male voters on a visceral level (her attractiveness perhaps balanced out her limited understanding of current affairs and her subsequent corrupt approach to government, made the McCain/Palin combo easy to defeat. No one wanted to think about Vietnam. And whereas Sarah Palin might have been eye candy for a certain demographic, the average American couldn't relate to her shotgun, moose-killing, politically rambling approach. She would be more at home on a Field & Stream hunting show than she would be in the White House.

We all look for certain non-verbal markers and codes when considering our concepts of leadership. For some people, the rough and tumble image of a leader such as Ronald Reagan, the cowboy who rides in on a white horse and talks plain while his doe-eyed wife looks on adoringly, resonates with that concept. In no case is it based in reality. Such codes we learn from movies, from magazines, from social media, from our families and peers, from our own spoken and unspoken codes about ourselves. We immediately feel relaxed and such codes are familiar—someone who 'speaks our language' or has our accent, organizes himself according to our social group, wears the kind of clothes we wear and does the kind of things we would do if we had the money, power, and prestige we see before us.

Pundits spend a great deal of time puzzling over the allegiance that rural America has for Donald Trump. After all, what does he really have in common with a redneck from Arkansas or a retired doctor from South Carolina?

First off, his fumblings are calculated, designed to create a code of familiarity for his base or would-be devotees. Many of them would be afraid to speak in public and, to see his fumbling for words, making off the cuff, cruel jokes at people who seem smarter than him, and otherwise speaking expemporaneously about his victories at the ballot box, at his private club, in the halls of power, creates a strange kind of resonance with voters who feel on the outside of society. (I.e., I might be a redneck from Arkansas but this guy gets me and all the intellectuals, wealthy people, bossmen, other politicians, and arch, liberal news media, they don't get where I'm coming from, but The Donald gets me). Trump encourages this with constant reminders that he's living the life his supporters would live if they were lucky enough to be him. He peppers his daily speech with superlatives, much like the trash talk you would encounter on a high school football field. He's irreverent. He spent a lot of time chatting about his sex life with Howard Stern, which exactly the kind of move some of his base would do if they were married to his third sexy wife and had access to all that money, all that power, all of the good life stretching right out in front of you to grab.

Secondly, his prevarication is designed to get you to agree with him and largely based on unfounded ideas that take on a life of their own. "Someone told me" and "I heard" and "I have the best sources on this, all the best words" are all concepts designed to create strength within his target group. He's an insider! He knows stuff we don't know and has access to things that we don't! Hence, not only should we trust him and believe what he says, but by telling us he's letting us in on a secret, which is exactly how we'd play it with our buddies were we to become president of the United States.

Finally, his code sharing anger at the media is aimed not at the reporters themselves (whom he loves. In New York he has a long history of tippoing off reporters, calling in to news shows, and otherwise keeping the media talking) but at keeping his base on tenderhooks and enraptured by his anger and indignation. After all, their understanding of complex geopolitical problems is very simple. Most look at the looming issues before us as simple problems, no harder than the way you cut off your 12th grader when he comes home with a beer in the back of the station wagon.

The feeling that the government of the free world, that international diplomacy, that centuries old problems such as the Palestinian issues, that our relationships with the Russians and China and North Korea can all be fixed by folksy wisdom is the greatest con game of our time.

Consider one conversation I had with a Trump supporter who was clueless as to why it was inappropriate for Ivanka Trump and Jared

Kushner to hitch along on AirForce One to attend Paris Fashion Week while Trump attended the G8 summit in Stokholm. "After all, he's her Daddy and was going anyway," they crooned. Why shouldn't she tag along? Making a trip to the tune of $200,000 involving a full security detail no more troubling than hitching a ride home from school with your best friend's Mom.

The interesting thing about code sharing is that our perceptions are so often wrong. Sharing a code doesn't mean you share the same values; you just know how to perfect the lingo and visual cues that let you into the in group.

Consider the fascinating case of the con artist David Hampton, who managed to con New York Society out of artwork and countless acts by kindness by pretending to be the college friend of the Park Avenue elite by perfecting their mannerisms, style of dress, and cultural markers. He bilked one couple out of thousands of dollars and was the subject of John Guare's fascinating play and the Will Smith movie, "Six Degrees of Separation."

The bottom line is we are all looking for people just like us. We all want to fit in. We all want to be appreciated and feel that we have one good idea (perhaps more than one good idea, if we're honest) that we think would change the world if someone would just heart us out.

But Trump's brilliance at code sharing is dangerous for the country in that it ignores everyone who doesn't feel the way he does or doesn't share the value of his code.

In June, when Trump was standing on the steps of St. John's, having tear gassed a peaceful demonstration to walk his dazzlingly white gang across the street and stand on the steps of a church that had he had only been in once, holding a Bible, looking to the sky for supposed divine intervention, meanwhile talking about how he is the 'law and order' president and that he would use whatever force necessary to handle an ever-increasing challenge with racial and political violence all across America, he was not sharing his codes of religion, reverence, power, and strength to bring an ailing country together. He was not wearing a mask, despite the fact that his own experts insist that as a best practice to protect vulnerable populations from COVID-19.

He was speaking only to his base, not to the people in the streets. He was strengthening his own power at the expense and, on occasion the lives, of those who do not share his cryptic values. He was having it over on us all.

It's time we demask him and the Republicans for what they really are— schoolyard bullies who will say anything, do anything to maintain their power base and hence their ability to loot the country of its remaining morals and rapidly dwindling wealth.

I'm wondering if Trump is familiar with that parable that Jesus discussed in his Sermon on the Mount. "The first shall become last. The last shall become first. And the weak shall inherit the Earth."

CHAPTER 3—THE MAN ON THE WIRE

Twentieth century newspaper impresario William Randolph Hearst once quipped, "I believe in the power of the press. The man who owns the press has the power." Here in the 21st century, in the era of sound bytes, the 24 hour news cycle, extreme vertical integration, the demise of the fairness doctrine, bloggers, 'influencers' and so-called 'citizen journalists' who are little more than amateurs with an iPhone and a lust for fame, the elemental concepts of power, politics and engagement present some very real challenges.

All communication, at its most basic, forms the nucleus of a struggle for dominance within a group. When Donald Trump stood in the Rose Garden in early June, proclaimed himself the "president of law and order" and continued "I recommended to every governor to deploy the National Guard in sufficient numbers that we dominate the streets. Mayors and governors, both established and overwhelming law enforcement presence until the violence has been quelled."
He was making a statement about power. More importantly, he was

making a statement not for the entire country, but a series of images and ideas that would energize and reinforce the beliefs of his base at the expense of those with whom he disagrees.

As always, there is what is happening on paper and what is happening in real time.

Even as Trump was giving this speech, he had deployed the National Guard to disperse a peaceful gathering of protestors in Lafayette Square using tear gas and rubber bullets so he could walk across the street, unannounced, stand on the steps of the St. John's Episcopal Church, and hold a Bible tenuously in his hand for a photo op.

Stronger groups are energized and reinforced by rhetoric that demeans or weakens the outgroup. Their definition hinges not on what they actually believe but on the polarizing difference between the two groups—we define ourselves by what you are not.

Hence, our perception begins to 'curve' in a convex way around us—we define the ingroup by the traits of the outgroup and the way we see the world becomes increasingly polarized against any difference. The goal is not to be welcoming or to bring people together. There is no 'why can't we just get along" or even the hope that people might start to understand one another. The strengthening of the power base is dependent upon animosity and difference, not engagement and collaboration. The power group does not need to collaborate with the outgroup to maintain power—all they must do is amplify and exaggerate the differences between the groups. That gets the job done and satisfies the in-group, whose identity originates not in their personal beliefs or a moral code, but in hating the 'other' that has expressed a different point of view.

This allegiance to bashing the other forms the basis of Trump's entire political strategy. Perhaps nowhere is it more evident than his rallies, which are vital to the maintenance of his power base since he has no other strategy for maintaining control, no other political platform, and no other agenda beyond escalating his power base and demeaning the outgroup. The ingroup's perception becomes more skewed and insular the longer this goes on without a viable challenger. Everyone else is playing a different set of rules. To the ingroup, all they must do is maintain the power they have by hating on the outgroup and skewing the ingroup's perceptions against the outgroup. The Republicans built this strategy on the birther movement, perhaps the ultimate gambit focusing on a possible 'outsider.'

This explains many things but especially why Trump, for all the things that he is, he will never be a conciliator or a president who brings diverse groups together. He's found a base. He panders to that base according to his beliefs which are, in turn, based on the sole notion of polarization—his 'beliefs' are the ones that polarize the outsiders and push them away from the center of power. The only way he can organize his power base and maintain it is by skewing their perception toward his ideas (the "convex perception") in which the insiders become increasingly insular at the expense of those with opinions outside of that perception. It is not an us against them paradigm. The insiders compile their entire definition based on what they are not— they are not 'foreigners,' they are not 'Muslims' (insert your spiritual paradigm here, but if it is not fundamentalist Christian, it would be on the outside), they are not liberals, they are not pro-choicers or minorities or the LGBTQ community or blacks or Asians or Mexicans or members of the G8 or the Chinese. The insiders believe that Vladimir Putin must be telling the truth because he, the former head of the KGB, one of the most ruthless espionage agencies in the history of the world, says that he is telling the truth. They believe Kim Jong Il, who has tortured the people of his own country during his entire reign of terror, because he and Trump 'have a good relationship and get along.' They believe Hilary Clinton was running a pedophile ring out of a Brooklyn pizza parlor. They believe that Joe Scarborough had a hand in the untimely death of one of his assistants. They believe that the Democrats are 'coming for their guns' and to squash their rights under the 2nd Amendment. They believe the students of Parkland School were paid actors. They believe that marauding droves of anarchists are roaming the streets of the United States. They believe that "there were good people on both sides" of the armed Klan conflict in Charlottesville, Virginia.

None of these beliefs are based on fact. None of these beliefs are based on a platform. Or a strategy that would leave the entire country forward.

Leading the entire country forward is not the objective of Donald Trump.

In fact, leading his base forward is not the objective of Donald Trump.

The objective of Donald Trump is to consolidate power and

pay lip service to a base that likes to craft their own policies and definitions around the concepts of what they do not think and how they hate the policies of the other side. They don't really have a policy of their own apart from that hatred and, any dissention is built on the notions of quashing difference and diminishing its power.

Quashing a different opinion reinforces the base in power and amps up the true believers who never question how things are going to get done or how things will be different if certain policies are put into play. All that matters to the ingroup is that their shallow beliefs are reinforced, that someone 'gets them' and that a leader seemingly sees things the way that they do. The fact that those things will not come to fruition in a concrete manner doesn't matter—Trump has become 'their president' simply by the virtue of voicing disdain for the other group.

General James Mattis, former Secretary of Defense, put it this way in a statement after the Floyd killing: Donald Trump is the first president in my lifetime who does not try to unite the American people—does not even pretend to try. Instead, he tries to divide us," Mattis writes. "We are witnessing the consequences of three years of this deliberate effort. We are witnessing the consequences of three years without mature leadership. We can unite without him, drawing on the strengths inherent in our civil society. This will not be easy, as the past few days have shown, but we owe it to our fellow citizens; to past generations that bled to defend our promise; and to our children."

This tenant of convex perception is what makes pejorative language so powerful in contemporary American politics. Thanks to the unwavering allegiance of vertical media outlets such as Fox News and right-wing pundits such as Sean Hannity and Rush Limbaugh, catchphrases become the touchstones for policies. Dissenters are labelled as 'snowflakes.' Former President Obama ("who might not even be an American, I don't know. Someone should look into that.") becomes a touchstone for supposed foreign Muslim terrorists who threaten to wreck the government and attack its institutions in much the same way that the terrorist attacks on 9/11 wrecked the national psyche and set us on a course with an imaginary enemy whose evil goals were destined to undo our society.

If you think of stereotyping and stereotypical language as shorthand for a nebulous belief system, then Trump's stronghold on his base and their rabid devotion seems more translucent.

The Trump presidency is not about improving the United States, though he once pledged that "You're going to win so much, you're going to get tired of winning." The Trump presidency's penultimate moment came when he won the electoral college. Everything that came after his defeat of Hilary Clinton on election night has been secondary to securing a position of power and, then, captivating his base and enraging his opponents. In doing so, he manages to ramp up devotion for his presidency and ideals as an abstract concept while demeaning the other side and rendering them ineffective. The more the outgroup tries to protest or defend themselves, the more they play into the ingroup's power. This is why Trump met national outrage over the killing of George Floyd with incendiary language and the proclamation that if the governors could not solve the problem of rioting in their states, he would mobilize the military and do it for them. This is why he has chosen to ignore the recommendations of his own public health advisors at the Centers for Disease Control and the National Institutes of Health, eschewing the wearing of masks in public and telling the governors of struggling states that "they're on their own.

Because they are.

One place this is most apparent is Trump's insistence that his daughter Ivanka, whose only credentials are running a shoe company that her father funded, and son-in-law Jared Kushner, a New York real estate hoodlum whose father went to jail for fraud, should be part of his inner White House cabinet.

Ivanka Trump is uniquely ill-suited to be a senior cabinet member of the White House administration, supposedly lending her expertise to issues relating to women's issues and public policy. Her influence is at best insular and clearly nepotistic. Though Ivanka Trump works in a 'voluntary capacity' and does not accept a salary, she has everything that the Trumps need for her to succeed---the power of the White House supersedes any public salary that could be offered. Ivanka's crashing ineptitude was best displayed in a video posted by the French government during the G20 in 2019. There, Ivanka, who attended as 'special advisor to the president,' looking like a winged confection in bubble gum pink couture attempted to make casual conversation with world leachers such as Angela Merkel and Justin Trudeau. The response from the room was reminiscent of being forced to indulge a host's three year old daughter who tells you about her unicorn dolls in her room.

In 2019, New York magazine writer Sarah Jones notes that, despite employing sweatshop labor in her China factories that drove many workers to suicide, the Trump administration is against the minimum wage. "I don't think most Americans, in their heart, want to be given something.

I've spent a lot of time traveling around this country over the last four years. People want to work for what they get," Trump said. "So, I think that this idea of a guaranteed minimum is not something most people want. They want the ability to be able to secure a job. They want the ability to live in a country where's there's the potential for upward mobility."

How ironic! Ivanka's potential for upward mobility came not in thanks to hard work or not getting what she worked for. Her potential for upward mobility and to attend meetings in the West Wing of The White House had everything to do with her famous father and his unwealing desire to make as much financial and political capital out of his time in the White House as is possible.

America is "doing very well," Trump added, claiming that her father's economic policies are "continuing to allow this economy to thrive." That'll be news to a lot of workers."

Far from being outraged with Jared and Ivanka's clear nepotism (Jared made a real estate deal in Qatar just a month before an official visit to the Middle East in 2017), the Trump ingroup sees such nepotism as what they would personally do if they were in such a position of authority. What's the problem with binging your daughter or son in law to work and getting them a good job?

Again, the ingroup doesn't care. They'd do it if they had the chance. The fact that we have laws that prohibit such things and seek to level the playing field, protect the environment, control international trade, pay living wages, address social and racial injustice and maintain our status on the world stage as a world power devoted to our traditional and legislative ideas means nothing to Trump and his base. It's not about fairness. It's not about enacting laws or regulating the rule of law. It's about cronyism. It's about skipping over a qualified person in favor of your daughter or your son in law. It's about using your own position to make money at your own hotels at the expense of fair dealing.

It was never about you. And the fact that you would like to enjoy your life, liberty, and the pursuit of happiness regardless of your ethnic identity, gender, education, or politics has been relegated to a dusty book in favor of a group of shameless, greedy thugs who are using the power of their office at the expense of the American people. It was never about you. It was about power. It was about money. It was about winning.

If you're in agreement, Trump throws you a bone that makes you feel good but will never benefit you directly.

It's exactly what you'd do if you were one of his followers, exactly the way you'd play it. After all, you're afraid of difference. You want to Make America Great Again, the America of the 1950s where you didn't have to have your ideals challenged and you didn't have to encounter people who were different than you. You didn't have to grapple with different languages, other political ideologies. You knew the rules. Men made the money. Women baked the cakes. Children knew their place. You could go over to a local plant and see your buddy or your uncle and he'd give you a job.

The even and balanced world, the greatness that Trump inherited, the one based on equity for all people, nurturing the environment, improving the economy, enhancing diversity, has been swept away in favor of every man for himself.

In the end, Trump's followers get nothing but a hollow belief that their moral superiority was just that—more and superior. History will prove otherwise.

After all, it's not about you. It's about him.

CHAPTER 4—TRUTH TO POWER

American poet Langston Hughes once wrote, "What happens to a dream deferred? Does it dry up like a raisin in the sun? Or fester like a sore-- And then run? Does it stink like rotten meat? Or crust and sugar over-- like a syrupy sweet? Maybe it just sags like a heavy load. Or does it explode?"

The United States of America in June, 2020 definitely feels the weight of deferred dreams and the resulting explosion. Thousands are rioting in the streets, demanding justice for a failed system of civil rights that has left many people economically, socially, politically, and morally adrift. President Donald Trump has chosen to meet public sentiment with militarization and inflammatory language, clumsily suggesting that citizens expressing both a lack of understanding of the United States' Constitution and a shocking propensity to attack citizens in what his Secretary of Defense termed "the battlespace."

If the public spaces of America have suddenly become 'the battlespace' in the eyes of the duly-elected president, then what is the next step? Anarchy? Bloodshed? Internment? Rage? A military state when the average citizen has no voice and hence no recourse and no access to justice?

We are better than that.

The thing to remember about convex perception and the outgroup phenomenon is that communication does not exist in a vacuum. It is fluid. It is not even a paradigm that is based purely upon winners and losers—it's all about the curve, bending the interest of people toward your ideas.

Trump's modus operandi in obtaining control and keeping it has to do with the use of language. He takes the shortcut typical of all bigots—a verbal shorthand that energizes those who feel that way in any case and alienates (and enrages) the people on the other side.

In schoolyards, this tactic is demeaning.

In civil society, it is the hallmark of the failed state.

How to react?

The first step is to first diffuse the powerbase of the stereotype. Ironically, this is not done by refuting the claims presented. If Trump says that the groups of peaceful protesters are behaving like "thugs" and must be controlled in "the battlespace," the knee-jerk reaction is to first prove otherwise. But just like that bully in 8th grade, asserting that you are not a chess-loving geek will not keep him from hitting you. In fact, trying to prove what you are not will only energize and strengthen the bully himself. He relies upon your weakness for his strength.

Stereotyping is all about perception. It is not reality. Thus it is futile to fight perception with facts.

The first step in changing the public narrative is to extinguish the stereotype itself. One does not do this by fighting back. This is done by failing to engage, one of the hallmarks of nonviolent resistance.

One thing about Trump and his administration. For all their idiotic ideas, they stay on message.

In mid-May, 2020, Donald Trump held a series of daily coronavirus briefings that quickly devolved into nothing more than campaign rallies for his base. At one such event, clinging to his ill-founded belief that COVID-19 could be managed by hydroxychloroquine (a theory that medical researchers have disproved), Trump announced to the media that he routinely takes the drug and has suffered no ill effects. As a rebuttal, Senate Majority Leader Nancy Pelosi noted that a person of Trump's age (73) and weight class (she referred to him as 'morbidly obese' whereas in reality he is classified as 'obese' would be in danger of the ill-effects of taking an unproven drug in an off-label manner.

When later asked about his response to Pelosi's comments, Trump remarked, "I don't respond to her. I think she's a waste of time."

Note the difference. Pelosi's comments create a push me/pull me argument that cannot be won, is off message (i.e., Trump's weight or his propensity for an unproven drug). It also deflects from the real issues that are supposedly important to his political rivals.

At this point, Trump is running roughshod over the American people and the international news media like a particularly nasty

Shetland pony with a bad combover that no one can manage and only children can ride.

His rivals forget their message in a maelstrom of nasty talk, innuendo, outright falsehoods and inflammatory speech. Don't think for a moment he doesn't know that he's lying. Don't think for a moment that he's saying what he's saying by mistake. And don't think that he's not laughing all the way to the Rose Garden as he consolidates power at the expense of the emotions of his rivals.

In making this argument about him, Pelosi played right into his greedy little paws. Her response shifted the conversation right out of her camp (health care, the failing American infrastructure responsible for so many deaths from COVID-19, Trump's unwillingness to following the guidance of the CDC and the NIH, his ongoing, maddening proclivity for public speculation or a thousand other things) and into his (simply put, his misguided belief that he knows best without any scientific evidence to back it up.

To his followers, this strengthens his base. Pelosi comes off as petty and weak. The perception (that word again) becomes that the Dems are picking on him, are sore losers, are weak.

How different would the curve be had Pelosi changing the narrative immediately back to the talking points of her party? "We're not interested in Trump's weight. What we do care about is the more than 100,000 precious American souls who have lost their lives because of the administration's inaction and misadministration of the Federal response to COVID-19 and our crumbling infrastructure that ensures that people will continue to suffer long after Trump loses the election in November of this year."

For all their flaws, the Trump administration is never off message. It might be a ridiculous message but it is not one that they ever abandon for anything else. As a result, the Republican base gets stronger and stronger while the Dems struggle to respond to their bullying.

Chairman Mao Tse Tung (I know this is a weird reference but bear me out) once said "A revolution is not a dinner party." So why do Trump's opponents continue to treat him as if he is their most treasured guest and not the traitorous opportunist that he has proven himself to be?

The first strategy is to bring the messages of disenfranchised groups, political leaders, governments ranging from local towns to Washington, and all opponents of his blatantly malignant administration into proper alignment. His opponents stand for justice. They stand for free speech. They stand for the rule of law. They stand for opportunity. They stand for the environment. To waste one second, one sound byte that could influence the election, one opportunity to sway public perception by indulging in the petty politics that only strengthen his base at the demerit of the country, is to be on the wrong side of history. Dr. Martin Luther King knew this. Malcom X knew this. Gandhi knew it. Benjamin Franklin knew it. And it's high time that the opponents of this administration get on the same page, focus on the talking points that they do know, and become consistent in their expression. If they do so, the ingroup phenomenon of Trump's outlandish promises and empty rhetoric will fade.

Facts won't necessarily get it done. But staying on message at the expense of the other party will.

Trump's detractors have often shook their heads in amazement at the people with whom he has associated and has brought on board (often very, very briefly, but that is beside the point) to rally his cause and enhance his voter base.

Perhaps none of these is more bizarre than the strange meeting that Trump held in the Oval Office with rapper, music impresario and Kardashian by proxy Kanye West.

In a ten minute exchange, the dueling sycophants discussed everything from Trump's love of professional athletics to Obama to Kanye's presumed devotion to Donald Trump and all that for which he stands.

In this telling snippet from their conversation, Kanye waxes poetic about the Make America Great Again hat and the relevance of Trump to his life in general:

"You know, they tried to scare me to not wear this hat – my own friends. But this hat, it gives me – it gives me power, in a way. You know, my dad and my mom separated, so I didn't have a lot of male energy in my home. And also, I'm married to a family that – (laughs) – you know, not a lot of male energy going on. It's beautiful, though. But there's times where, you know, there's something about – you know, I love Hillary. I love everyone, right? But the campaign "I'm with her" just didn't make me feel, as a guy, that didn't get to see my dad all the time – like a guy that could play catch with his son. It was something about when I put this hat on, it made me feel like Superman.

You made a Superman. That was my – that's my favorite superhero. And you made a Superman cape."

As a thinking person, you must be thinking right now, "what the hell?!" And you'd be right.

As a communications theorist, I'm thinking that Kanye's meeting with Donald Trump was a slam dunk for the Trumpian ingroup at the expense of the Democrats. Note the connection—how many people in America come from a one-parent household, are longing for their father, love rap, are African-American, or even like Superman (though I must express here a strong preference for Batman, to each his own).

The second tool in the anti-stereotyping toolkit is the long-used and much-heralded two step flow theory. Developed by sociologist Paul Lazarfeld and elaborated by communications researcher Elihu Katz in the mid-50s, the two step flow theory suggests that communication is not a linear theory (which is also called the 'magic bullet' or inoculation theory). People do not necessarily hear a message through a medium (television, radio, the newspaper, online sources) and then act directly upon their message without further intervention.

The two step flow theory suggests that people are influenced by act by opinion leaders that the recipients perceive as authoritative and valuable. Hence, a message is delivered by an opinion leader that the group perceives as credible or important and then message is then acted upon based in large part to the reverence in which the group holds the messenger delivering the message. Two step flow is a hallmark of contemporary advertising and, more recently, the key element in the rise of media 'influencers.' If you want to 'be like Mike,' wear Nikes. If you want to be glamourous, find an influencer you admire online and take their advice and do what they do.

Trump was hitting on all cylinders with Kanye West. He's African-American. He's a rapper. He's a Kardashian. His associations make him an unlikely proponent of Donald Trump but his demographic profile make his pronouncements valuable. And to people who would like to be like him, with money, prestige, talent, a sexy wife, mansions, and a previous dalliance with Pamela Anderson, his opinion matters. In that respect, he's possibly credible to a certain demographic (though one wonders if anyone asked who that might be, exactly). And that credibility translates to credibility for Trump by mere association.

Again, it's about perfection, not necessarily reality. And any student of the Trump presidency will notice that it is a very thin group of celebrities and public opinion leaders (if you remove Fox News, Sean Hannity, Rush Limbaugh, and a gaggle of conspiracy theorists from the equation) who stick around for very long. The fact that they have endorsed Trump at all is somewhat astounding.

Trump himself attempts to employ two step flow with measly results. Hobnobbing with international thugs such as Vladimir Putin and Kim Jung Un. Cozying up to border-wall-loving extremist groups and the xylitol-variety white supremacists in his own cabinet. The challenge becomes that more people believe in Trump than take their cues from the people he has swirling around him. After all, does Pat

Robertson's word or Franklin Graham's devotion really entice anyone to do anything?

It also pays to consider that Trump's base makes their decisions largely upon emotion and how he makes them feel (like a rebel! An innovator! An outsider!) coupled with the stereotypes that make them feel both comfortable and in touch with their own values. Hence, his catchphrases have a lot of meaning to his base both as symbols and philosophic constructs (who could argue against the notion of Make America Great Again, though one would be hard pressed to define one way in which Trump has brought that omnipresent slogan to fruition)?

The defeat of Hillary Clinton had a lot to do with these perceptions and her campaign's utter failure to successfully tap into the celebrity endorsements and opinion leaders that could have influenced the electorate. By considering her a lock on the nomination and underestimating Trump's ability to mobilize the largely white male demographic with whom his message resonate, Hillary Clinton failed not only to connect with young women voters who were logically excited about the prospect of a woman in the White House, she also made choices that alienated the vote of Middle America, whose support was critical to winning the White House. To be fair, Hillary Clinton won the popular vote and lost the electoral college vote. It is likely that Russian interference damaged the election of 2016 and paved the way for Trump to enter the White House. However, Hilary did little to distinguish herself from her husbands' presidential term, fell victim to the right's aggressive onslaught of innuendo about everything from the death of Vince Foster to the illuminati, and never crafted her own talking points until Trump's momentum had overwhelmed her candidacy.

Two step flow theory depends on the target group's perceptions about opinion leaders—it is not who you feel is important or who is actually important, but who they validate within their group as important. This allowed such political non-entities as Kid Rock to lend his name to the Trump campaign and invigorate his base. A segment of rural America idolizes Kid Rock (again, that outlaw notion) and Trump was able to capitalize on that perception to influence a much-needed demographic.

To win the upcoming election, Trump's rivals must carefully identify the opinion leader in their target group. Again, that leader might not be readily apparent. For example, Barbara Streisand was a famous supporter of Hillary Clinton—but did many people actually vote for Hillary because Barbara was doing so? Probably not.

Finally, it is vital that the outgroup have an understanding of the reference symbols that translate into power in the American psyche and use those symbols to solidify their power base without deflecting their message, their opinion leaders or their symbols to the other side.

Referent power is when a subject attempts to captivate an audience by associating or affiliating with symbols, concepts, or ideologies that the target group already perceives to be powerful. This was the purpose of Trump's use of the military to clear Lafayette Square and walk across the street from the White House to St John's Episcopal Church for a photo op in which he clumsily held a Bible aloft while posing for photos with a few senior members of his cabinet. This act was not about the photo op itself; it was a statement to the church, a reference that his Christian voter base could assign as relevant. He said nothing to make it relevant. In fact, all he did was hold the Bible and glare into the camera. But in that act Trump managed to align himself with the notions of Christianity and faith, the mistaken concepts that the country was founded on Christian ideology, and the nonverbal gestures of a strongman in the time of crisis.

By the following day, Trump was comparing himself to Lincoln and his press secretary, Kristin McAniny was comparing his gesture to Churchill's wartime walk through a bombed out London. So how does the outgroup counter such images?

One way is consistent reliance on the imagines that resonate with voters and yet distance themselves physically from Trump. There is power in diversity, power in the Constitution, power in the institutions of the government that uphold the rule of law. However, in a time when some such institutions, such as the police, are held under scrutiny for their corruption and failure to promote unity, there is also an opportunity for the Democrats to seize the moment, re-identify the images of referent power that speak to inclusion and progress, speak truth to power outside of the toxic and base dialogue that Trump perpetuates in an effort to maintain control.

We all look to the context and syntax of words, of gestures, of totems and symbols as we attempt to craft our beliefs and make sense of an increasingly senseless world. Our sacred spaces and personal beliefs are often at odds with the messages around us. This does not mean that we cannot reach out and create new meaning or that we are doomed to the recidivist thinking of the parties of oppression. We must understand the strife and pain that such symbols and antiquated thoughts have caused to those around us. We must act with compassion and according to a philosophical code that goes behind the photo op and the sound byte for its context and significance.

When Dylann Roof killed the members of a Bible study group at Mother Emmanuel AME Church in Charleston, South Carolina, he walked straight in the door with murderous intent. The members did not know him. They did welcome him according to their faith, according to their belief system, not according to the fear that he would have hoped to instill in subsequent generations. Their behavior was built on a foundation that went beyond symbolism. Its home was the heart.

The Trump era is tremendously challenging for the people of the United States and the world. As treaties are broken, social contracts demolished, symbols appropriated, and language relegated to nothing more than media circus, we must remember that we are more than the messages around us. We must seek to understand the context of who we truly are as a nation, the bedrock of our Constitution, the intent of our founding fathers, the innovation of our leaders who changed society to make our country more inclusive for all its citizens, a place where each person can enjoy "life, liberty, and the pursuit of happiness" without the fear of repercussion or the challenges of tyrannical, self-serving leaders.

The great poet Alice Walker put it this way,

"love is not concerned

with whom you pray

or where you slept

the night you ran away

from home

love is concerned

that the beating of your heart

should kill no one

The 'battlespace' is not a park across from the White House. It is in the heart of every American. And we must decide the merit of our convictions and examine the context of our ideals if our country is to survive.

CHAPTER 5—FROM THE EXOTIC ORIENT

To better understand the cultural, racial, economic, and political schisms that confront the American people, we must first have a clearer concept of how people accumulate information and then use it make decisions. How do we 'know' what we know? And how do we then act on the things that we know and those bits of information to make decisions? How does our knowledge color not only the way we see the world but the manner in which political figures and other opinion leaders approach us and attempt to present information that will move us in a certain direction to take political action or strengthen the aforementioned 'ingroup' at the expense of an existing 'outgroup.'

My Vietnamese friend often recounts an experience from her freshman year at a large university. While at dinner with some of the women from her dorm, the conversation quickly turned to her native country and flawless English. She politely explained that, while Vietnamese by birth, she was raised by American parents in Minnesota.

"What do they speak in Minnesota," one young man inquired. My friend explained that, though the official language of the United States is English, many people speak Scandinavian languages.

"Like Vietnamese," the young woman asked. My bemused friend responded that Vietnamese is an Oriental language while Scandinavian languages include Danish, Swedish, and Norwegian.

"So you're Norwegian," the dinner companion exclaimed.

"Ya (yes)," my friend replied. "I just couldn't teach the whole world to her."

This small anecdote says much about the misplaced reference points that confront us all and presents an endless challenge as we strive to communicate with one another. At its most elemental, communication is a series of shared reference points. It might be commonality in language. It might be a shared cultural identity. It might be geography. But we all have to connect on some footing to truly 'get' one another. My friend should have explained the cultural, historic, and economic differences between the various Scandinavian countries to her university colleague, the time investment was a waste. There was no common ground upon which they could have a meaningful conversation. At the least it was a lost opportunity on the part of the young woman who didn't know that Minnesota is part of the United States.

In the late 1980s, educators such as E.D. Hirsch, Jr., and John Timbaur, along with researchers at the National Geographic Society and the Brookings Institution, began to examine the cultural literacy of American students. The difference between what people should know (or should be taught) and what they actually do know is staggering.

Benjamin J. Stein writes that, in his experiences with Los Angeles teenagers,

> I have not yet found one single student in Los Angeles in either college or high school who could tell me the years when World War II was fought., Nor have I found one who could tell me the years when World War I was fought. Only two people could tell me where Chicago is, even in the vaguest terms.
> On and on it went. One and on it goes. I have mixed up episodes of ignorance of facts with ignorance of concepts because it seems to me there is a connection. The kids I saw (and there may be lots o others who are different) are not mentally prepared to continue the society because they basically do not understand the society well enough to value it.

In my research, I focused upon the segments (or sectors) that comprise our understanding of our society. What are the factors that contribute to the decline of our base of knowledge about our own country, the one we need to live here, the one we must have in order to be intelligent consumers, good citizens, engaged voters, full participants in our democracy?

Psychologist Charles Pierce suggests that individuals make use of four ways of knowing or fixing belief, namely:

1. Tenacity: Holding to what is true because 'it has always been true';

2. Authority: Holding that something is true 'because an authority says so';

3. A priori: Intuitive knowledge before the fact;

4. The scientific method: An objective look at a piece of information dependent upon one or more of the following objective processes:

A. Deductive reasoning: Logic that progresses from the general to the specific.

B. Inductive reasoning: Logic that digresses from the specific to the general.

C. Rationalism: An internal source of knowing

D. Empirical reasoning: An approach emphasizing knowledge that comes through factual investigation, with the facts discovered through sources external to the investigation; and

E. Monothetic set: The structure of a theory in which data or results from studies are logically linked together to form a theory.

Though the principles of tenacity and a priori knowledge have their place in communications theory, their primary utility lies in the role that they play in stereotyping. They are not of chief concern when looking at the role that the media play in the acquisition of factual knowledge. After all, the tenacity and a priori principles center on the distortion of facts and perceptions of those facts rather than how they were initially acquired.

The Scientific and Authoritarian schema concern those of us who study communications paradigms for two reasons: first, the role that the media play often puts them in the ad hoc position as an authoritarian figure (i.e., we must act because Rush Limbaugh or Anderson Cooper says it is right) and, secondly, the media are often the informative source that voters use in an informal, unstructured form to make decisions in their daily lives.

Hans Speier has reduced the Authoritarian Schema to the following paradigm:

Speier notes that if the recipient is ignorant, prejudiced, or superstitious and the communicator is knowledgeable, the recipient acquires knowledge from the communicator and is thus enlightened.

But what if the communicator presents inaccurate information to the recipient? If so, the resulting information is either intentionally or unintentionally considered disinformation.

Just as Trump carefully stays on message at the expense of the facts, understanding the theory behind that communication is key to understanding not only his base of supporters but how they filter and process the official party line from the White House and shape their world view accordingly.

Though it would be wrong to characterize Trump's base of support as fully ignorant, they are complicit in accepting the messages that he overtly presents as fact and, more importantly perhaps, the process that they use to evaluate the meaning of such messages and subsequent actions that must be taken.

Consider the strange success of Trump's slogan "Make America Great Again."

MAGA is an excellent example of how people create meaning by holding to the notion of things that have 'always been true,' tenaciously fixing their beliefs in spite other methods of creating meaning that might provide a more balanced view of the world. The official MAGA hat is available only via the Donald J. Trump website, along with other slogans such as "Keep America Great" and MAMA, hats for babies (magaBABY) and "Blacks for Trump." Though these hats are made in the California, the Chinese have had a brisk business selling knockoff hats for the secondary markets.

To be fair, the MAGA hat is ironic and pretty much has everything that a symbolic totem should have to influence a base. It's a cheerful red. It's technically a 'trucker hat,' not a ballcap, which appeals to the working class roots of the ingroup. It's made in America. The direct message is that America is great, as echoed by Trump himself. The tenacious sense of 'permanent truth' is a little more problematic. What about people whose historic experience of America has been anything but great? The descendants of foreign slaves, for example, who never wanted to come to America in the first place and are now, rather than crafting a revisionist, tenacious sense of what the country is, see the possibility in crafting something new?

As far as the MAGA symbol goes and the people who tenaciously cling to it, there is no room for an outgroup that believes that America is anything but great. The ingroup crafts meaning based on the notion that America was (and is) great. The context of that meaning, obviously, does not need to be built on a messy tower of facts, it can be crafted out of thin air, evolving from the individual's experience. And if you think that America was great because it was an all-white America or an otherwise segregated America or an America where your thoughts and beliefs, imperfect though they are, take precedence over the rule of law, then the MAGA hat fits in perfectly to the way your group constructs meaning and the ways you think about contemporary American politics. You don't need facts. You don't need to know what other people are thinking. You don't even need to know, directly, what's in the Constitution in order to use the tenacious method to create meaning for yourself. Believe it, and it is so.

The problem with MAGA in general is that it assumes that stasis is perfect, that we don't need to move forward. This slogan increases the power of the ingroup at the expense of the outgroup. So you don't think the America of 1950 or 1965 or even 1990 was perfect? Then to hell with you. The ingroup's experience gets stronger and stronger. Your experience is paramount. And facts are stupid things. No communication occurs in a vacuum. There are dependent, intervening variables you can see. And dependent, intervening variables that are hidden from view, the things you cannot see and can never know.

Make America Great Again on its own is not a bad slogan. Not everyone who chooses to wear a MAGA hat is a bad person. Trump uses this vagarity to his relentless advantage and MAGA is just vague enough to give license to a wide berth of bigots, racists, conspiracy theorists, white supremacists, and miscreants of all stripes.

Consider the strange example of an elderly man in Palo Alto, California who was assaulted in a local Starbucks for wearing the MAGA hat.

A heated confrontation over politics in a Palo Alto Starbucks on Monday has gone viral nationwide, leading to reported death threats and also calls for greater dialogue and empathy. It began when Palo Alto resident Rebecca Parker Mankey attempted to shame an elderly white man wearing a red Make America Great Again hat as he sat in the coffeehouse — an encounter she later wrote about on social media. Calling him a "hater of brown people," Mankey said she yelled at him and addressed Starbucks customers and employees to join her in her effort. She said she left the store but soon returned and continued to yell at him. Mankey said she was "heartbroken" that other white people didn't stand up against the man sporting a slogan that was popularized by Donald Trump during his 2016 presidential campaign. She followed him out of the store to the parking lot, where she continued to berate and swear at him.

She called the man "Nazi scum" and threatened to post pictures of him on social media, which she then did, along with her version of the incident on her Facebook page and on Twitter. She asked the public for help finding him — "I want him to have nowhere to hide," she wrote -- a practice called "doxing," or posting personal contact information to encourage threats and harassment.

The incident has had repercussions not only for Mankey, who said on Tuesday she's received death threats and was fired from her job as an accountant, but also for her former employer, Gryphon Stringed Instruments. Staff at the store said they were inundated with angry phone calls and emails Monday and Tuesday.

Why are people confused by the meaning of a hat and its symbolism? And what prompts us to create our own meaning when there are other methods that would allow us to take a different approach and come to more inclusive conclusions?

Trump uses his bully pulpit to energize his base. He's not big on facts. He's big on the visceral response he gets from the people at his rally. His messages incite an emotional response among his supporters and, as evidenced above, also an emotional response from those who disagree with him.

The fact that the New York Times can fill their editorial pages with the lies that Trump has spoken in public since his inauguration in 2016 is irrelevant to voters who are constructing their own sense of meaning using a tenacious mindset. The facts only get in the way. And Trump doesn't need the facts to influence this portion of his base— they are influenced by their own perceptions and totems of the way things were and the way they could be again. They don't need the reality of others to Make America Great Again in their own minds.

The Trump Revisionism has little to do with a longing for the Good Old Days; they are merely using this tactic to propel the support of their base forward, win elections, and hence recraft the government in a manner that will allow the wealthiest 1% to make more money at the expense of the 99. The Good Old Days are veiled by the prospect of a bigger payoff for a minute group in the future.

Tenacity is the hallmark of systemic racism, failed opportunity for women, and an immigration policy that favors the notion of an all-white America and the nebulous threat that outsiders are "here to take your jobs." It is predicated upon emotion, not fact. Tenacity allows people to willingly or unwittingly misconstrue the relevance of the Constitution and the historic intent of the Founding Fathers. It allows the Conservative Religious Right to conveniently skip over the provisions of the First Amendment that ensure the separation of church and state while clinging to the misguided belief that Jefferson and the framers of constitution were Christians and built the government upon Christian ideology.

The construction of a tenacious worldview allows Trump to strengthen the ingroup by using what they don't know against them. They don't know the facts apart from their emotional response to it. More dangerously, they don't want to know. It's good enough for them to be mired in ignorance and making decisions accordingly. And it's certainly good enough for Trump, who panders to his base at the expense of unifying the country and upholding the Constitutional rights of all people.

The Trumpers love to look back to the Good Old Days, the ones that they tenaciously hold too, the America that they held close to their dreams, the America that never was.

The purpose of this statement is not to say that every person who voted for Trump has constructed a worldview via tenacious thinking. Granted, there are other reasons and many people have made sense of his narrative in other ways highlighted in Pierce's theoretical hierarchy.

The hat wearing people, the ones who scream epithets at his rallies, the ones who cheer as he mocks people with disabilities or jeers about fake news or tolerate his misogyny and isolationism, the ones who believe Barack Obama is an ISIS operative or that Hillary Clinton was running a sex ring out of a Brooklyn pizza parlor, these are the same people who want the old world back. They want an old world that is all white. They want an old world where women 'know their place.' They want an old world full of US manufacturing at the expense of globalization. They think the World Health Organization and the Gates's Foundations initiative to cure pandemic diseases are a liberal plot to compromise their health. They stood by, silently, with glee in their hearts as Trump spewed his hate-filled rhetoric noting that "when the looting starts, the shooting starts" after the murder of George Floyd. They believe that a border wall between the United States and Mexico is as logical a solution as putting up a wire fence to keep rabbits out of their gardens. Again, the ingroup sees Trump's backward looking policies and think they will transport them, like a time machine built out of the old Trans Am they had in high school, back to the days when 'life was simpler' and the only citizens who mattered were the ones who thought just like them. When a rapist could be nominated to the United States Supreme Court and his crimes could be brushed aside as "a boy being a boy" against a woman who had it coming. They don't have to wear a mask against a deadly, novel global pandemic that has killed millions of people around the globe because they think it's all a big conspiracy by a global power to bring down their ultimate authority, Donald Trump. They eschew facts for feelings. They think masks are for sissies. When the President said he'd grab a woman he wanted by the pussy, they cheered.

When Vladimir Putin says he didn't interfere in the US election, they believe him because, really, why wouldn't they? He seems like a good guy. He rides a horse without a shirt.

The 'trouble' with creating your own history out of your own fond memories of the way life used to be is that, just as the writer Thomas Wolfe once noted, you can't go home again. It was never a place to begin with and, even if it was, your memories are as flawed as your elementary school geography textbook and all the superstitious nonsense that was believed before the scientific theory and the true, clear authority of facts became relevant in the here and now.

Slogans are generally a dangerous thing. They are a shortcut to thinking for yourself. And having a motto that someone else crafted in a marketing campaign, a motto that will yield the spokesperson billions of dollars while you sit, poor, grappling with your diabetes and struggling to pay for your insulin or get your son some treatment for his opioid addition or find a job for which you are qualified while the world races ahead, is a gambit that only benefits the designer of the motto at the expense of everyone else.

Think on this while you're wearing your MAGA hat, watching

riots on television, as innocent people bury their loved ones and all that Trump could do in response was order law enforcement to fire some bullets on an innocent group of peaceful protestors exercising their First Amendment rights. Think on this as he clumsily grips a totem sacred to you, a Bible, the one you held your hand on when you got married, the same book you might have found comfort in when your Mama died or when you got the news you're your brother was killed in Afghanistan.

Hang tenaciously to the reality you have created while the whole world burns.

As you do so, Trump's ingroup is hanging on to their ideals as well.

They're not looking back to the Good Old Days. They're raking in the cash in the here and now

CHAPTER 6—SNAKE OIL

Twenty Nineteen was an interesting year. Hurricanes ravaged the Gulf of Mexico. Wildfires swept through California. The summer was hot, miserable, full of emotional challenges for people who watched the news with a kind of anticipatory horror, the sort of feeling one gets when you're at the movies and know that the lead characters should not go into a dark cellar and yet know in your heart that, inevitably, they will.

One day in 2019 I was waiting in line at the bank my small southern town while two people, one of them a teller and the other her customer, discussed the news of the day. "They say that all this bad weather is because the people in California passed that law that lets gay people marry," one theorist intoned. "It's God's punishment."

"It is!" the teller agreed. "The preacher said it in church." And thus it must be so.

To thinking people who use the scientific method to organize meaning, this seems like a ridiculous exchange, as implausible as seeing a unicorn while visiting the post office or riding a magic carpet home. And yet, the authoritarian construction of meaning—in which a person builds their belief system, their actions, and their political choices around their devotion to a perceived authority--has very real consequences in the Era of Trump. It enables wishful thinking. It creates a polarized social dichotomy where you are either right or wrong, ignoring the grey area in which most political decisions and the variable, ever-shifting borders of the truth that governs our lives, resides.

Stereotyping depends upon thin veneer of symbolism, not fact. It is a kind of mental shorthand that people use to elude the very real and very challenging work of making sense of an increasingly senseless world. Our fumbling attempts to develop our own moral code depends on the things that we can assess and the meaning that we can 'organize' in the 'real world.' Much of this organization comes from direct experience.

For example, I personally am terrified of snakes.

It is a fear that is utterly out of proportion to the danger that snakes present to humans. Most of this terror comes from my direct experiences as a child, when my father bought a large property in the mountains of North Carolina and spent the afternoons after work clearing the wilderness to make pastures for a horse farm.
These activities meant that snakes were often present in the debris and I was warned to stay well out of harm's way because of this. I have never had a close encounter with a snake. I am so afraid of them that I cannot even watch them on television. No one over-reacted or gave

me warnings out of proportion to the danger that snakes present to the average person walking in the woods. I have used my experience to organize, both consciously and unconsciously, my opinions.

The way that I organized what I know about snakes (my stereotypical thinking and resultant out of proportion fear of them) was also reinforced by a message from a person that I considered an authority (my father, whom I adored), though his advice was not extreme or out of line with the danger that snakes presented (after all, he was the person directly dealing with the possibility of protecting me from snakes, while I was sitting safely in a Jeep).

To put it in a paradigm that expands upon Pierce's theory previously discussed, my thinking about snakes is a combination of the strategies that all people use to create meaning and express it.

Though I would like to use the scientific method to organize my thinking, but much of what I know and how I think about snakes falls squarely in the a priori construct. Not the best way to think about the facts and certainly not the best method to use when putting together a response to something in the natural world.

Even though I learned about them in school and even had the benefit of a family that loved the natural world and sought to educate us on the wonders of nature, despite the fact that I have, as an adult, walked through the woods in the company of PhDs in biology and science educators, I am still terrified and certain that I hold a number of incorrect notions about them.

Consider, now, how different my fear would be, how intense it could become, if an authority figure that I admire consistently communicated to me that snakes were far more dangerous than my experience leads me to believe and if I were willing, either through ignorance or preference, to ignore organizing what I know in terms of the scientific method and went with the authority figure's belief.

One of the most influential theories of power was developed by Bertram Raven and John French (French & Raven, 1959; Raven, 1992). Raven identified five different types of power—reward power, coercive power, legitimate power, referent power, and expert power. Raven and French argue that each type of power exerts a different type of social influence, some creating public compliance and others creating private acceptance.

These are:

- Reward power: the ability to distribute positive or negative rewards.
- Coercive power: The ability to dispense punishments
- Legitimate power: Authority that comes from a belief on the part of those being influenced that the person has a legitimate right to demand obedience.
- Referent power: Influenced based on identification with, attraction to, or respect for the power holder.
- Expert power: Power that comes from the observer's belief that the power-holder possesses superior skills and abilities.

When we look at Trump's presidency through the lens of Raven & French's power paradigm, we are met with inconsistencies that lead to some startling conclusions concerning his leadership of the United States and the subsequent constructs that his devotees use to make sense of their citizenry, their fellow countrymen, and the world.

The position of President of the United States is the most powerful public position in the world.

As such, the people of the United States, through their Constitution and subsequent rule of law, have established the authority of the office and rights and responsibilities to the office bearer. This is legitimate power in one sense, duly elected by the people of the United States. The manner in which the people respond to the power of the authority figure holding the office, and how that authority figure chooses to wield the personal eccentricities of his or her office (the 'leadership style,' if you will)

We are all are also working on an internal versus external continuum. At one end we have our private thoughts; at the other, what we are willing to do publicly to express our allegiance. All authority figures manipulate this continuum, some more than others.

The problem with Trump is that he lets his private thoughts and lust for power spill out into the real world.

Recently, there was a public debate about whether Trump prayed or not when he stood on the steps of the St. John's Episcopal Church in Lafayette Square holding a Bible as if it were a small token of his admiration, a small little symbol that such a powerful person would be likely to hoist on such an occasion.

Higher than the people, only slightly lower than the angels. To the right hand of God Almighty, perhaps.

It was a familiar gesture to students of history, of whom Trump appears to not be one. He considers himself more of a modern reformer, though has lately been comparing himself not only to Lincoln but to Churchill, thus showing that he is no student of history. There are no photographs of Hitler holding a Bible in front of his adoring acolytes. The fact that people took to the internet to find out if that was true (and that I had to verify the possibility when writing this one) says a lot about the imagery that Trump employs, what it means to his base and the extremist elements within that base, what it says about his divisiveness and the symbols that he employs and the meaning of those symbols outside of his own context.

What does it say about the possibility of the future when the sitting U.S. president holds up a Bible and people immediately think of Hitler.

Nothing good.

Donald Trump is a garden-variety bully who happens to hold the authority of the President of the United States. He claims that the people elected him in an overwhelming majority; they did not. He won by electoral college in an election that was heavily influenced by the Russians.

Trump loves dictators. He loves the imagery, the classical imagery of potentates, all that gold leaf and marble and the penthouse views of great cities, everything slick, polished, cool and controlled, the leader scowling knowingly from behind an overdone gold desk. He likes control, as any aficionado of "Celebrity Apprentice" will readily tell you. He likes the overdone trappings of power, the hyperbole, the helicopter that squires you around Manhattan, the cool bottle blondes that fawn over him while he throws a tiny bone to the public that admires him.

That's why an actual, dangerous dictator such as Vladimir Putin appears believable to the U.S. President. It's a kind of hero worship, the one that hopscotches over silly things such as the Constitution, voter's rights, and the dignity of the people in favor of cheap photo-ops, inflammatory speech, rubber bullets, and general mayhem.

He does not want it to calm down.

The only way he can maintain control is by keeping the country at such a fever-pitch that thinking people can't think, his base can have the opportunity to spew further hate and make wild assumptions out their fellow citizens, and, every now and then, he'll have some 'bad guys' use some rubber bullets on some 'other bad guys,' stroll across a street in the District of Columbia, hold a book with which he is blissfully unfamiliar, and send a message to his followers both benign and dangerous.

Putin would do this differently.

The issue with Trump's love of totalitarianism is that it discounts and diminishes the Constitution, blurs the lines between the three branches of government, and makes the seat of power in Washington a global laughingstock.

Geopolitics is not a zero sum game. There are implications to every action. The workings of foreign policy take decades to put into place and conflicts that have festered for generations are not solved by sound bytes or the novel thinking of a failed American real estate magnate with a penchant for a mocked-up version of Versailles and a tennis pavilion for his failed model wife in place of an organic garden.

Before long, he'll be suggesting that his own scowling mug be stamped upon a gold coin.

And his base, ignorant of history, enamored of hate, willing to give up their own civil liberties to 'keep the bad guys out' of the streets, turning up at his sycophantic rallies to rail insults against Hillary Clinton and only talk about the news that they like, will go along with enthusiasm.

The thing about symbols and stereotypes is that, in the hands of people who make their sense of the world via facts, they are ridiculously weak and unseemly in comparison to the systems of power that are already in place. They are a shortcut where one group wrongly demands privilege at the expense of another---hence "good guys" with guns can patrol the street whereas "thugs" can take to those same streets to express their First Amendment rights of free speech and lawful assembly.

The demise of the Fairness Doctrine, the rise of social media where every person with an iPhone and a grudge considers themselves a citizen journalist, and the actual journalists are berated from the most influential seat of power in the world for doing their jobs, means that consumers only have access to the news that they like. And the news that they like involves the demolition of others.

Trump is using the trappings of power, the tv reality star version of power, to manipulate the weakest, poorest educated, and most vulnerable voter base in modern times.

If Fox says it, it must be true. If Newt Gingrich or the formerly drug addled Rush Limbaugh throw their credibility behind it, that's enough for his base. They only want news that validates what they're already thinking.

Such thinking opens a Pandora's box of conspiracy theories, all enthusiastically embraced by Trump and his advisors. Why suggest that Barack Obama is not a US citizen? Why suggest that journalists are peddling fake news? Why utter so many lies behind the great seal of the President of the United States that newspapers run out of ink trying to publish them all? Why insist that household bleach or an unproven drug for lupus can somehow wipe out the deadliest global pandemic of modern times? Why be relentless in blaming others, taking no responsibility for the office to which he was elected. Why does the buck stop somewhere over there.

One reason is that doing so fits the reality star image of what a strong person would do. Because when Trump rails against the governors or hates on the mayor of Minneapolis or ignores the advice of the world's leading authority on infectious diseases, he's doing so from the vantage point of an image-only leader. All he wants is the image necessary to help his base keep him in power, those poor souls huddled around their smart TVs eating Cheetos and drinking Pepsi, making the wild assumption that Trump probably really did say a little prayer when he was standing on the steps of that church, a gesture that, according to the president, "Franklin Graham and a lot of religious leaders loved."

I bet they did.

For all his occasional, flinty-eyed proclamations of the love of religious right, Trump doesn't talk a lot about the Bible and hadn't appeared actually in St. John's Church since the day of his inauguration. When a reporter asked him that day if the Bible he awkwardly held aloft was his own, he remarked, "It's a Bible." He didn't elaborate.

Snakes appear a lot in the Bible. The snake tempted Eve with the promise of eternal paradise and one poisoned apple that Christians believe ultimately unleashed a world of fear, sin, disease, and death upon the world.

When the prophet John the Baptist accepted God and was baptized in the Jordan river, some legalistic Sadducees and Pharisees were on hand to witness the event. The two groups were warring for political and social control at the time. They would go on to eventually crucify Jesus. In the Bible, which Trump conveniently did not read or reference but is revered and followed by millions around the world, the writer remarks,

> *"But when he saw many of the*
>
> *Pharisees and Sadducees coming*
>
> *for his baptism, he said to them,*
>
> *"You generation of vipers, who warned*
>
> *you to flee from the wrath to come?"*

Time marches on. Empires fall. Controlling groups change and are lost to the dusty pages of time.

The vipers remain.

No matter who you are, facts present a crossroads critical to your worldview. To quote that most unlikely of American Nobel laureates, Bob Dylan, "It might be the devil or it might be the Lord but you're gonna have to serve somebody."

And at any crossroads, you have a choice.

You can investigate. You can accept the source as credible and believe a fact as truth. You can investigate and stick to your initial belief despite the presence of evidence to the contrary. Or you can choose to stick with your belief, accept your incorrect source as credible (despite the fact that they are wrong), and doggedly stick to your misguided belief with all the stubborn resolve for the truth.

Ronald Reagan once famously misquoted a speech by John Adams, saying, "Facts are stupid...I mean stubborn things." The Oxford Dictionary of Quotations outlines the Reagan's misquote of President John Adams thusly

Often represented as a misquotation by Ronald Reagan of the words of John Adams (second President of the United States), defending soldiers in the 'Boston Massacre' trials in March 1770.

In the course of Adam's speech he said,

"Facts are stubborn things; and whatever may be our wishes, our inclinations, or the dictates of our passions, they cannot alter the states of facts and evidence."

In his address to the 1988 Republican National Convention, Ronald Reagan introduced a section of his speech with the words:

Before we came to Washington, Americans had just suffered the two worst back-to-back years of inflation in 60 years. Those are the facts, and as John Adams said, 'Facts are stubborn things.'

This paragraph, and the following four paragraphs, finished with Adams's words. However, at the end of the third paragraph, Reagan made a verbal slip, which he immediately corrected. A transcript of the speech reads,

'Facts are stupid things – stubborn things, should I say. [Laughter].'

Trump's blatant disregard of the truth and the stubbornness of facts will go down in history as the greatest con game ever perpetuated by the United States president. He is, put simply, a pathological liar. Some of it clearly by design. Some of it clearly by his proclivity for speaking off the cuff without the benefit of notes and data. Some of it designed to enhance the ingroup at the expense of the outgroup and to permanently discredit reliable sources. Some of it is a culture of lying that Trump had done all of his life, according to biographer

Gwenda Blair, who noted in the New York Times that

> *Trump looks for people who share his disregard for the truth and are*
> *willing to parrot him, "even if it's a lie, even if they know it's a lie, and*
> *even if he said the opposite the day before," said Gwenda Blair, a Trump*
> *biographer. They must be "loyal to what he is saying right now," she said,*
> *or he sees them as "a traitor.*
>
> *Campaign aides often echoed Mr. Trump's pronouncements knowing they*
> *were false. People joined the top levels of his administration with the*
> *realization that they would be expected to embrace what Mr. Trump said,*
> *no matter how far from the truth or how much their reputations suffered*
> *("Mueller exposes the culture of lying that surrounds Trump" by Sharon*
> *LeFraniere, The New York Times, December 1, 2018, Section A, pg.*
> *1).*

To be fair, the New York real estate business is a high stakes game, a combination of bluster and brinkmanship. It's cutthroat.

To make money, the Titans of Manhattan sometimes display a bravado that would make P.T. Barnum look like a moderate man.

In that respect, Trump's lies in the White House echo his behavior throughout his professional career in Manhattan. The stakes, however, involve not some prime real estate in one of the richest cities in the world nor a cushy golf resort in an exotic locale, but the well-being and freedom of the entire world.

It is, in short, unbefitting a sitting president to lie to the American people, more akin to the behavior of a third rate dictator. Why Trump lies is not important; that must be left to history. Many academics and journalists and professional pundits and even armchair cowboys will spend the rest of their lives trying to figure that out.

Frankly, I don't care, and you shouldn't, either. Do we really have time to dig into the festering, bewildering, small minded Coronavirus has killed more than 100,000 precious souls in the United States alone. More than 40 million people are thus unemployed. Many businesses are shuttering never to reopen. Millions are rioting in the streets as a response to the senseless murder of George Floyd in Minneapolis by a police officer and the country's relentless, needless, systemic racism. Millions go to bed hungry, afraid, worried, unemployed, drug addicted, on the street, grappling with the ever-crumbling infrastructure of our roads, our public buildings, our overrun courts, our poorly funded schools, now empty thanks to COVID-19 but even before that withering away to dust with disheartened teachers, bewildered administrators, and aging curriculum as Secretary of Education (and googly-eyed billionaire) Betsy DeVos rides that already wet horse into the ground.

All that matters is how the perpetual lying of the Liar in Chief affects the life, liberty, and pursuit of happiness of each and every citizen in America. And how can the people, who, after all, are paying for this parade of mendacity on Pennsylvania Avenue, understand what happens and choose to steer the rapidly sinking, rat infested, gold-digging ship in a different direction before it capsizes altogether?

To some people, truth is not paramount to the ways in which they construct meaning or make sense of the world. Just as the tenacious constructors cling to the notions of Make America Great Again, the authoritarian constructors assign the meaning to messages based on their confidence in who said them. This explains Trump's near-magnetic hold within his devoted, Republican base. He is everything they want in a President: possibly rich, possibly affable, possibly savvy in the ways of the world, staunch about his beliefs in gun rights and anti-abortion and seemingly conservative on the issues that they treasure. He looks like their idea of an authority, just as Reagan's square shoulders, slow manner of speech, and love of cowboy hats crafted an image of sort of The President as John Wayne that appealed to many uneducated voters.

Michael McQuarrie, associate professor of sociology at the London School of Economics, notes that Trump's victory in 2016 depended upon the change of heart among less educated working class voters in the 'rust belt' of America, voters whose jobs had been depleted by trade policies and to whom Hillary Clinton's geeky, academic rhetoric had little appeal. Thus, the 2016 election was secured by voters who were less educated, more emotionally engaged with Trump's message, and felt that his economic policies had more resonance with their everyday lives. (albeit vague and, admittedly, most of those policies were never realized once Trump was in office).

McQuarrie notes

Many important questions emerge from this. How do voters get from Obama to Trump? What role did racism and misogyny play in flipping people from the Democratic to Republican columns? These are important. But the character of the communities that flipped must be grappled with. These are communities that have been suffering from neglect and decline for decades. Families have gotten poorer and there are few opportunities for people who stay. The people who voted for Trump are very willing to overlook Trump's abuse of women, Muslims, and people of color, and that is to be condemned.

Some percentage of these voters are ideological and practical racists and misogynists. But explaining the electoral shift from someone who stood for the opposite of those things to Trump is impossible without considering the communities where these voters reside and what the candidates offered them. White people generally didn't deliver the White House to Trump, however much they enabled him; the Rust Belt did. And unless we are attentive to the economic factors involved, as well as the social and attitudinal ones, we leave open the path for future demagogues to exploit the same set of circumstances in the name of securing political power ("Trump and the revolt of the rust belt," American Politics and Policy, London School of Economics, November 11, 2016).

Currently, though Trump remains strong within his base, uneducated voters outside of his base are having second thoughts about voting for him in 2020. Trump has often referred to this demographic publicly (his famous "I love the poorly educated whites" comment while campaigning in Nevada) and it turns out that the 'poorly educated,' especially women, are now having second thoughts about voting for him in 2020. A recent Pew validated poll of voters in 2016 noted that

Overall, whites with a four-year college degree or more education made up 30% of all validated voters. Among these voters, far more (55%) said they voted for Clinton than for Trump (38%). Among the much larger group of white voters who had not completed college (44% of all voters), Trump won by more than two-to-one (64%

to 28%).

Understanding voter preference and behavior is a complex business. The COVID-19 pandemic, economic collapse, and civil unrest creates a challenging environment for researchers.

Regardless of their preferences in 2016, it can be reasonably assumed that less-educated voters create meaning in a manner that can easily be outside of the use of statistics, factual data, and hard evidence. Trump uses this to his powerful advantage and such voters were largely responsible for flipping the election in his favor in 2016. To win in 2020, he must do this again, which might be a very hard sell among voters who have suffered economically, socially, and educationally in the meantime.

What has not been a hard-sell for Trump is his propensity to craft meaning and pass along his words of wisdom to an uneducated base who have neither the resources nor the educational background to make judgements in light of the facts presented before them. Consider the strange interplay between how Trump presents facts to the country and the facts of the COVID-19 pandemic.

Dr. Anthony Fauci was appointed director of the National Institute of Allergies and Infectious Diseases in 1984. He oversees an extensive research portfolio of basic and applied research to prevent, diagnose, and treat established infectious diseases such as HIV/AIDS, respiratory infections, diarrheal diseases, tuberculosis and malaria as well as emerging diseases such as Ebola and Zika. NIAID also supports research on transplantation and immune-related illnesses, including autoimmune disorders, asthma and allergies. The NIAID budget for fiscal year 2020 is an estimated $5.9 billion.

Dr. Fauci has advised six Presidents on HIV/AIDS and many other domestic and global health issues. He was one of the principal architects of the President's Emergency Plan for AIDS Relief (PEPFAR), a program that has saved millions of lives throughout the developing world.

When COVID-19 hit the United States in 2020, Dr. Fauci routinely presented updates, gave interviews, and discussed the significance of the coronavirus with the media. His expertise and factual discussions of the ever-escalating virus in the United States put his public appearances at odds with President Trump's propensity for speaking off the cuff, speculating aloud, and downplaying the dangers of the virus during its initial stages.

As of this writing, more than 107,000 people in the United States have died as a result of COVID-19. Meanwhile, Trump floated out an incessant string of falsehoods from the White House. He stated that "like a miracle it will just go away." In fact, many of Trump's statements, disproved in the popular media using data from the CDC, the NIH and others, formally challenged in the press by experts such as Dr. Fauci and the World Health Organization, have only been designed to delude his followers, strengthen the stereotypical thinking and authoritarian constructs of 'reality' that he must hang on to if he is to win in November.

He cannot win with facts. He cannot win by leaning on experts with decades of experience in epidemiology. He cannot win by taking a look at where we are now and attempting to use those experts to craft a logical way forward. He cannot win by telling the truth. His ingroup has zero interest in the truth. And they, the economically disadvantaged, the poorly educated, lack the ability to interpret data and understand the experts.

What they do understand is news that makes them feel good. And, barring that, news that supports the ways in which they process information and understand the world around them is preferable over a disease that is scary, hard to understand, impossible to prepare for and deadly.

Trump responds emotionally when reporters challenge him with facts. He yells "fake news" at them and appeals to the base that prefers conspiracy theories to reality.

If the news is fake, then why are the funerals so real?

CHAPTER 8—LIES, DAMNED LIES, & STATISTICS

I n his book, ***Chapters from my Autobiography***, published in 1907, American humorist Mark Twain wrote,

Figures often beguile me, he wrote, particularly when I have the arranging of them myself; in which case the remark attributed to Disraeli would often apply with justice and force: 'There are three kinds of lies: lies, damned lies, and statistics.

The explosive popularity of social media, the internet, and the ability to create meaning and information in the virtual world flooded with newspapers, magazines, television, video on demand, websites, the highly vertical aspect of newsgathering, the 24 hour news cycle, influencers and freelancers, is perhaps the most significant game changer in the realm of media, politics, and power.

In the early 2000s, I attended a high level meeting hosted by the Online Publishers Association in Atlanta, Georgia.

There in the sylvan conference room at the top of the Atlanta Journal Constitution building, while nibbling on a typical southern breakfast and fortified by cups of (then quite unique) Starbucks Coffee, a group of nationally recognized newspaper editors looked at data and puzzled over the possible role that the burgeoning online culture could play in the future of the newspaper business.

How could the internet be monetized? How could the media connect with consumers who increasingly wanted their kind of stories in their own timeframe, apart from the fairly rigid schedule of the publishers of daily newspapers? There was discussion of paywalls, websites that would complement print content, and sponsored content in which companies pay for their products to be featured in legitimate news outlets such as newspapers, magazines, television, online pop-ups and popular films.

"We know there's a way," said one speaker. "But we're not sure what it's going to be."

A lot has changed in twenty years.

These days, any person with a phone, throughout the world, considers themselves a would-be reporter. If something happens, they whip out their phone, photograph what's going on, and post it on Facebook, Twitter, Instagram, Tiktok, YouTube or any number of platforms.

I once was travelling along the Silk Road in Pakistan, thousands of miles from an organized city, in the shadow of the highest mountains in the world. We stopped to get fuel. A man approached the car and we had a small discussion about a much-heralded, currently happening cricket match between India and Pakistan. He then pulled out his phone and checked the scores in real time.

This real time aspect of news is both a blessing and a curse.

In one respect, the free flow of information means that the public gets to see much that would never have been seen otherwise. Reporters cannot be everywhere at once. It also means that news, misinformation, bias, advertising, and countless other bits of information are constantly flowing toward consumers who may not possess the skills needed to evaluate well-crafted messages from those with either hidden or blatant bias.

Trump's incessant 'fake news' epithet is diametrically opposed to the procedures, methods, and theories that most professional journalists apply to their work. Journalism is, after all, the Fourth Estate, considered the fourth branch of a democracy (the three being the Executive, Legislative, and Judicial branches of government). Journalists are crucial to the continuing survival of the United States of America. Without reporters and accurate reporting, the public is left at the mercy of the powers that be, with access to only the information that they want the public to know, presented only the best light for the presenter. Without journalists, there is no one asking questions or speaking truth to power.

In their book, ***Key Concepts in Journalism Studies***, BOB FRANKLIN, MARTIN HAMER, MARK HANNA, MARIE KINSEY & JOHN E. RICHARDSON explain the role of the media as the fourth estate as follows,

> *Classical liberal theory views the press as a defender of public interests and a 'watchdog' on the workings of government. The term originated in the eighteenth century, gained ground during the nineteenth and even now*

generates debate. It is derived from the notion of 'estates of the realm'. The traditional three are the Lords Spiritual (clergy that sit in the House of Lords), the Lords Temporal (other peers) and the House of Commons.

It's been attributed to several thinkers and writers including Edmund Burke, Richard Carlyle and the nineteenth century Times leader writer Henry Reeve. In October 1855 Reeve wrote in an article in the Edinburgh Review 'journalism is now truly an estate of the realm; more powerful than any of the other estates' (in Boyce et al., 1978).

The argument runs that the press plays a central but unofficial role in the constitution because it helps to inform the public of issues, articulates key concepts, as well as public opinion and therefore can guide and act as a check on government. (O'Malley, 1997).

But it can only fulfil that function if it is independent and free from censorship. Described as arrogant and grandiose by some, and satirized in an 1855 novel The Warden by Anthony Trollope, the notion refuses to lie down and die. As one of the ways of expressing the relationship between journalism and society, it still has ideological resonance.

As recently as 2001, the BBC's political editor Andrew Marr wrote in the Independent 'If people don't know about power and let their attention wander completely, then those in power will take liberties' (Franklin, et.al., Key Concepts in Journalism Studies, Sage, pg. 84).

We live in a time of unprecedented media saturation, something that the framers of the Constitution and even the developers of the 'fourth estate' concept could have never imagined. When George Floyd was murdered by a Minneapolis police officer in early June, a citizen took a film. The entire world saw the unedited footage. It was easy to draw conclusions, some just and some unjust, based on what one 'saw' online or what a friend shared on Facebook. But, just as different angles show different scenes, the public debate rarely centers around the best practices of journalism, how one separates accuracy in media from inaccuracies and falsehoods, and what a journalist is actually doing when they are doing their job well. It is the responsibility of professional journalists to speak truth to power. The higher purpose is to 'stand in' for the concerns of the public, asking questions and conducting investigative reporting so that the public can be made aware of the issues, policies, and relationships that are relevant to life. The Fourth Estate is, by its very definition, antagonistic to those in positions of power and authority. If they were not, how would they be able to impartially evaluate the situations, politics, and policies around them?

I have worked in newsrooms, at newspapers and magazines, as a writer and professor of journalism for almost all of my life. At the age of 10 or so, I founded a small newspaper for the street where I lived in a small North Carolina town, typed it out by hand, and placed it in the mailboxes of all the neighbors on the street. The 'paper' was filled with stories I thought were important to the community—how to feed birds, the reports of the summer vacations of other school children my age who lived on my street, recipes from the community's great cooks, public service stories about upcoming events and classes offered by the town.

My first job at a newspaper, where I was sent to cover a youth club cookout and write a small story, was when I was 13 years old. My Mom had to drive me to work. The editor of that newspaper, incidentally, is one of America's celebrated experts on community-driven journalism, a professor at the University of North Carolina at Chapel Hill, and a lifelong advocate of the importance of local news in a democracy.

At family gatherings, my aunt would set up a small typewriter and stack of typing paper so I could do real-time reporting of the goings on.

I was, in short, a geek in love with the concepts of the news. I still am.

I was privileged to know and study with some of the best media experts and working journalists in the world. I have worked both as a researcher and a writer for national magazines and newspapers. I graduated with a masters degree in journalism research from The University of South Carolina, where my mentor was a former editor at Newsweek and winner of the Pulitzer prize. I received countless accolades for my work relating to the issues of media, politics, and power.

For the most part, journalists are not out to trick you.

We have protocols relevant to our work. We adhere to ethical guidelines that are traditionally established for our profession, guided by editorial committees, enhanced by our own sense of right and wrong. We strive to be impartial. Some reporters do this better than others, but the tenants of our profession demand that we attempt to get it right, find the best information we have at our disposal, connect with the best experts we can find, ask questions that are well-framed and in the public interest. Our ethics demand that we not accept compensation from sources, personally stay out of politics, and not lobby for our own private preferences in public. This means that we pay for our own meals when we review restaurants; buy our own tickets when we go on travel stories upon which we intend to write; and keep our personal noses out of politics at every level. We look for depth in sources. We adhere to deadlines and post corrections and retractions when we get it wrong (we're human, after all). But we are not out to trick you. We just want to our jobs well. We want to make a difference in society. We believe in the values of the Fourth Estate and its relevance to the machinations of our government. If we don't stand in for you, how will you know what's going on?

Granted, we're no longer living in the era where Thomas Paine is setting each letter of type by hand. In fact, everyone's a journalist. Newspapers traditionally separate opinion from news content. And yet, newspapers often clearly endorse certain political candidates and their viewpoints on their opinion-editorial pages. And, of course, editorial columnists clearly label their viewpoints as such.

The media explosion has increased what media researchers call 'verticality' in the presentation of news. If you're conservative, you might get your news from a conservative source, such as Fox News. You're comfortable with their content because it aligns with your own. If you're more liberal, you might favor CNN. Again, the content, the editorial commentators, tend to mirror your own perspective.

This is not inherently a bad thing. In fact, the demise of the

Fairness Doctrine, in which news outlets were forced to present both sides of an issue by the Federal Communications Commission, has been roundly criticized as censorship. Most of the programs that were presented to comply with FCC guidelines (think of "Point/Counterpoint" on CBS's 60 Minutes, for example) have made their way to the vaults of time. People shouldn't necessarily be forced to listen to both sides of an issue; we should know enough and have the freedom to consume those sources for ourselves.

In a free market society, people should be free to choose their own news sources, even if the viewpoint of those sources is something with which you vehemently disagree.

And so, what of Donald Trump, the authoritarian wanna-be, who wants strongman photo-ops with tanks rolling down Pennsylvania Avenue as he stands, admiring the military hardware of the greatest country on earth? Who uses military force to clear protestors (who, incidentally, were exercising their first amend rights of free speech) from a public park so he could stand, scowling, in front of an historic house of worship?

The problem with Trump and his 'fake news' gambit is that it ignores the beauty of the United States Constitution and the role of the fourth estate in the checks and balances of power. It is as if he is attempting to convince his power base that the media don't matter, that the only news that is relevant is the news that is favorable, glowing, ass-kissing.

You really believe that? Then perhaps you didn't see the entire editorial page of the New York Times filled with a chronology of

Trump's lies?

Trump's dalliances with the Russians as evidenced by the Russia problem and the subsequent debacle concerning his supposedly quid pro quo with the Ukrainians throw his sense of absolute truth into some dispute. What is not in dispute is that the media have a right to ask the hard questions, under the Constitution, and the fact that Trump neither likes those questions nor spends a proportion of every meeting with the press attempting to discredit their work in the most emotional, authoritarian, tenaciously recidivistic manner possible issues of the Russia problem and subsequent debacle concerning the Ukraine draw the absolute truth into some dispute.

To be fair (that word again), not everyone weighing in on the issues of the day is a professional journalist. As professionals, we give credence to the 'sources of record' that have a long history of verifying sources, long relationships with both named and unnamed sources in the halls of power, and the ability to separate fact from opinion.

Trump doesn't even pretend to do this. He prefaces every question that he doesn't like in front of every reporter with "you're fake news! No one likes you! That's why my ratings on 'Celebrity Apprentice' were stronger than Anderson Cooper's ratings on CNN." "Nobody likes you?" Sound familiar? Remember the 8th grade bully? News reporters do not have to be liked to be respected. If you consider that it is the role of the media to be antagonistic, what would you have them do. True leaders should be able to stand up to questioning. There are no embarrassing questions, only embarrassing answers.

In 2018, President Trump had the press credentials of CNN senior White House correspondent Jim Acosta revoked after a particularly heated exchange in which Acosta refused to let go of a microphone while asking a question with which the President disagreed.

The exchange invoked outrage among the press corps, the White House Press Corps Association, and media watchers throughout the world.

"The president should not pick and choose who covers him, and he should certainly not force out a representative of one of the country's leading news organizations, one that tens of millions of Americans depend on for their news," said Elisabeth Bumiller, the Washington bureau chief for The New York Times.

Olivier Knox, the president of the White House Correspondents' Association, urged the White House to reverse its decision.

"The White House Correspondents' Association strongly objects to the Trump administration's decision to use U.S. Secret Service security credentials as a tool to punish a reporter with whom it has a difficult relationship," he said in a statement. "Revoking access to the White House complex is a reaction out of line to the purported offense and is unacceptable."

"Difficult" is putting it mildly. There is long-term evidence to suggest that Trump actually loves the media. Before he became President he was a frequent call-in guest to radio shows around New York, frequently on Howard Stern's radio show, and pretty much spent a lot of time tipping off the media as to his whereabouts and upcoming projects.

Trump's media strategy is relentlessly on point. And it's objective is simple—undermine the credibility of the media with his voter base (remember the largely uneducated fan base that won him the election by flipping the vote in the rust belt, the vote that went to Barack Obama in 2012). All he has to do with voters who are largely uneducated and relatively unskilled in evaluating media messages and making sense of meaning apart from the scientific method and factual reasoning. The Trump administration makes no attempt to value the checks and balances that the media provide to voters; they feel no obligation to provide reporters or the public with accurate information. In fact, the crazier, the better for a fan base that wants to believe they are in with the in crowd and on the right side of history despite the evidence to the contrary. This feeds into conspiracy theorists. It gives rise to the belief that legitimate reporters with legitimate credentials are no more credible than a teenage influencer hawking Juicy Couture from her dorm room bunk bed. It establishes a culture that erodes the necessity of legitimate information and replaces it with dreck.

The information that comes from the White House press briefing room paints the daily machinations of the Trump administration in such glowing terms that you would fully expect Vladimir Putin to jump out from behind a curtain and join into the proceedings. The information is shameless, riddled with inconsistencies, largely rhetorical in a daily meeting that is designed to present information. During the COVID-19 pandemic, not a day has gone by without Mike Pence's unrelenting, boot polishing pandering to the President and his supposed excellent judgment.

In early 2020, Trump attempted to absolve himself of any responsibility for his administration's mishandling of the global onslaught of COVID-19. He routinely disparages women, minorities, and reporters with whom he disagrees. His base feeds on these allegations, crying out fake news at every story they don't like, assuming that things are the fault of 'the liberal media' and college professors and secret societies and anyone else with whom the current administration disagrees.

Secretly, or perhaps not so secretly, Trump would like to silence the media. That way, his uneducated base could further believe his elaborate lies. There would be no one to stand up to him. And the only news would be happy news.

From that vantage point, that podium high above the rule of law, redesigning the government in his own image and taking his vainglorious, pomposity to the next level would be a piece of cake. And it would be, to quote Trump, the best chocolate cake you've ever had in your life.

CHAPTER 9—DON'T TREAD ON ME

In 1730, my fourth-great grandfather, Benjamin Andrew, was born in the Dorchester Colony near Pon Pon, South Carolina. A planter, he eventually moved to the settlement of Midway, Georgia and owned a large agricultural plantation near Colonel's Island, Georgia. He was a contemporary of southern revolutionaries such as Lyman Hall, George Walton, and Telfair, was named the president of the Council of Safety, was a delegate to the Continental Congress, and later, a Congressman from the State of Georgia. He was one of the original Sons of Liberty, a secret society founded by John Adams to oppose the Stamp Act.

In the Spring of 1773, the British naturalist William Bartram travelled down the east coast of the colonies to make note of the flora and fauna of the Carolinas and Florida. He visited my great-grandfather at his plantation on Colonel's Island with the purpose of learning more about the cultivation of rice. In his book, Bartram's Travels, he notes that "I arrived at the seat of the Hon. B. Andrew, Esq., who received and entertained me in every respect as a worthy gentleman would a stranger, that is, with hearty welcome, plain but plentiful board, free conversation, and liberality of sentiment. I spent the evening very agreeably and the day following (for I was not permitted to depart sooner) I viewed with pleasure this gentleman's exemplary improvements in agriculture, particularly in the growth of rice."

By 1776, my great-grandfather's house had been burned to the ground by the British army. He and his family moved to August, Georgia, where he served as Congressman.

Though they were represented by several flags during the time of the Revolution, the Southern delegation of the Sons of Liberty often were represented by the popular Gadsden Flag, pictured below. It's a yellow flag with a coiled serpent and the phrase, "Don't Tread on Me." Gadsden designed the flag in Charleston, South Carolina around 1733. It was one of the many flags used by the Sons of Liberty.

Even though it's more than 250 years old, you might be familiar with the Gadsden Flag. And, like most flags, its meaning is fluid in context. In recent years, the Gadsden flag (which, you must admit, looks pretty cool and very nice on a T shirt), has experienced something of a resurgence at the hands of Tea Party activists, anti-government types, Second Amendment proponents and other activists. Rob Walker notes in a 2016 feature in The New Yorker

Along the way, it picked up other connotations: strident anti-government sentiment, often directed with particular vehemence at the first African-American President. As the E.E.O.C. gingerly suggested, the symbol is now "sometimes interpreted to convey racially-tinged messages in some contexts," citing the flag's removal from a New Haven fire station after a black firefighter complained, and a 2014 incident in which two Las Vegas police officers were killed and their bodies covered by the flag. (The officers were white, but the shooters reportedly "spoke of white supremacy" and "the start of a revolution," and were presumably sending that message with the flag.) Other skirmishes around the flag's display, largely centered on its association with the Tea Party, have entangled small businesses, homeowners' associations, and even an empty building. "People who collect historical flags like to fly them occasionally," John M. Hartvigsen, president of the North American Vexillological Association, says. But some have shied away from "historical display" of the Gadsden flag because "it can now communicate a political sentiment that may not be theirs" (Rob Walker, 'The shifting symbolism of the Gadsden flag,' The New Yorker, October 2, 2016).

I live in a small mountain town in western North Carolina, in the heart of the Bible belt, in the heart of Trumpland. I drive by at least two of the Gadsden flags in a two mile section of road near my house, just outside my town of approximately 500 loyal Trump supporters, both flying aloft, all alone, on flagpoles in the front of single-wide trailers set in the woods.

Slightly further afield, along Interstate 40 near Charlotte, North Carolina, one sees enormous Confederate Battle flags flying atop 50' flagpoles near the Interstate, on private land, for all to see. Note that this attention, the reverence, for the Confederate flag--lighted at night, blustering in the breeze throughout the day, hundreds of feet in the air, flying presumedly at a private residence whose occupant wants to send a clear message to the thousands of travelers who drive that route every single day.

My county, McDowell County, is one of the poorest counties in the state of North Carolina. Here, far from the sophisticated banking centers of Charlotte and the high-tech biotech of the Research Triangle Park, people are bereft of both meaningful employment and basic technology. High speed internet is unavailable outside of the limits of the two small towns where I live—there are many, many schoolchildren in my county who have no access to healthcare, no access to high speed internet to do their schoolwork during the sheltering in place orders caused by COVID-19, many people who have never travelled outside of their home state. The 45,000 residents of my county are largely white (92%). Thirty percent (30%) lack broadband access. More than 80% do not have a college education; of those, 30% did not graduate from high school. Almost 20% live in poverty.

My county, with its shabby trailer parks inhabited by meth dealers and pit bulls on chains, with its unloved children playing in the dirt, miles from the information superhighway, huddled under the banner not of an American flag nor of a military flag but of a 250 year old flag of revolution or a 130 year old battle flag that represents oppression to almost 46 million Americans, is ground zero for Donald Trump and the Republican party.

In the recent local election, the Republican candidates all won handily because the Democratic party, who do exist and are active of

Facebook, meeting every month or so at a Chinese restaurant to whine about the lack of Bernie Sanders, failed to put up even one local candidate for the open seats.

Barack Obama made a swing through my county in 2011. He stopped at a local barbecue restaurant, his modus operandi for the bus tour (and, as you might imagine, barbecue being the beloved food of all North Carolinas, perhaps the only thing upon which all people could agree). The Republican sheriff of my county was dining in a small dining room off the main lobby in the tiny restaurant but did not come out to meet the president. Several people said, "I don't like him but it's good to see a president anyway."

Donald Trump carried more than 75% of my county in the 2016 election.

For all the would-be patriotism of the rural south, the shiny, patent-leather veneer of the Bible belt reigns supreme among the God-fearing, poverty stricken, uneducated and unemployed people of the rural South. The county-council in my local town is currently fighting a new business, a brewery that had recently invested millions into a crumbling Main Street, because the town aldermen do not want to approve beer sales on Sunday, citing a law from the 1800s as their precedent.

It would be easy to make some wild assumptions about the people all across America who are living in such communities, the rural poor, the uneducated, the drug addicted, those people who have to choose whether to buy another case of ramen noodles or a week's worth of insulin.

I think the clear understanding of the issues they face—and the type of reporting that they receive at the hands of the national media—is largely absent from the national dialogue about the meaningful way forward.

Sure, the press might visit my community. The New York Times even did a feature on the demise of the textile factory around which the town is built, the nearly 800 jobs that were lost when 'the plant' closed and the textile finishing industry moved overseas. They might write a small snipped about the changing business plans of a company such as furniture manufacturer Ethan Allen, whose recent bankruptcy and restructuring closed one of the main points of pride in my small community, where many people have houses full of upscale Ethan Allen furniture as a result of their involvement in the now-defunct North Carolina furniture industry.

So when the White House press secretary stands on a podium and says, as she did yesterday, that a new day is dawning, I know she's not talking about my community. I know that Donald Trump will never visit to have a look at the small businesses that a new generation of people are struggling to build, the ones that supplant the crumbling mills, the ones that serve hand-crafted beer or the small art gallery or the small beds and breakfasts and might entertain tourists who visit the mountains for adventure and relaxation.

The thing to remember is that the people of my county, the ones who would not come out of the back dining room of a small barbecue restaurant to see the first black man elected as President of the United States, the ones who pray on Sunday and think beer is a fast track to the devil, the ones who don't have internet, who live in a small single wide trailer next to a meth addict and let their kids play in the dirt in the front yard, these are the people who elected Donald Trump. He has their support. And, when the fast-talking, well educated, worldly by comparison Democrats across town show their possible love of multiculturalism by talking politics in a Chinese restaurant and yet fail to deliver one single candidate to the local election, it is certain that the Republicans and all that isolationistic talk of American jobs and America First and Make America Great Again resonate with this base of voters. And while the liberals and the ideologues twiddle their thumbs, the Trumpers are using the power of symbols, the rhetoric of hate and isolationism, to fire their guns from the shoulder of those who don't know any better, the uneducated whose idea of an ultimate vacation would be a condo at Myrtle Beach for a weekend, a round of golf, and a cooler full of beer.

It is a message that resonates with the outcasts. When they see Donald Trump, they don't see a slick, would-be billionaire with a nude model wife, a gaggle of blondes in his wake, a man so confused and convoluted and, frankly, unschooled in the issues of geopolitics, economics, history, health care, and the rule of law that he has brought an entire cadre of frauds, hucksters, opportunists and gold diggers right through the front doors of 1600 Pennsylvania Avenue.

Rather, his voter base sees a guy who 'gets them,' who was fun to watch on The Apprentice, who Is reshaping the culture in his own image thanks to a media that focuses on sound bytes rather than context. They love it when Trump yells at the media, 'fake news!,' because his behavior echoes their own frustration with a media system that talks down to them, relentless in its stereotypes, utterly irrelevant in its approach to the concerns of their neighborhoods and the reality of their lives.

My family came to America with the Jamestown Landing in 1607. They forged their way into the New World, despite disease, war, and unrest. My mother grew up on a large cattle farm in South Carolina, a farm now run by my cousins who attended universities, worked as engineers, travelled the world and always came back home to the farmhouse built by my great-grandfather.

Every year, we collect at a brick schoolhouse that my grandfather built for the people of the community. There, we attend the small Methodist church (our ancestor, Benjamin Andrew, was also the grandfather of Benjamin Osgood Andrew, one of the founders of the Methodist Church in America), visit with our cousins and enjoy 'dinner on the ground' at the small, two room schoolhouse. There, with the creaking wood floors and the leaded glass windows, we tell stories, visit with our aging relatives, and always take a walk out to the cemetery to look at the gravestones of our relatives. It's a very rural sort of tradition, eating fried chicken in a small schoolhouse, laughing with your aunties and uncles about their upbringing, coming home.

The classic painting of George Washington, the unfinished portrait, hangs above a pot bellied stove near the chalkboard. I used it sit and wonder about this unfinished portrait, the wooden teeth of the first President of the United States, all that amazing imagery and whether it was true---the cherry tree, crossing the Delaware, the elder statesman of a new country in a (new to them) world.

Though our family's riches seemed to evaporate centuries ago, we were never uneducated people. We understood our history, from the time of Jamestowne, from the rice plantations of Benjamin Andrew, through the Civil War, the World Wars, Vietnam, and Iraq. We attended universities, worked hard, got good jobs. My mother and her sisters, despite their upbringing in a rural corner of the Upstate of South Carolina, could all quote Shakespeare at length, understood history, read books, saw the world. They worked hard but were also capable to seeing the world as it really is.

The challenge with Trump is that he is conning an electorate that barely has the same advantages that my family enjoyed nearly two hundred years ago. He knows you don't know history and the history, the sacrifice, the theoretical constructs of this country don't matter to him. He knows you won't go look it up if he states an outright lie in front of you on television. He knows that you don't have the education, the context, the long view of the history of this country, the one that is essential to know that Don't Tread on Me is not just a cool yellow flag that might make a nice T shirt. It is not an emblem of hate. It is an emblem of sacrifice. An emblem of people, actual founders, the actual living human beings who carved this amazing democratic experiment out of a marshy wilderness and, steeled by that resolve, brought freedom, the rule of law, and a way of life around the world. It is devastating to see the ideals of our democracy brought low by petty thugs and self-serving messages of division and hate. It is devastating to see so many people suffering in what was the greatest country of earth, the one that others looked to for inspiration and hope in the times of great darkness, the one whose innovation and resolve truly did change the world.

How sad it is that, in this time, our uneducated fellow citizens, themselves frustrated and disenfranchised by a government that only sends them checks, not solutions and a media that gleefully stereotypes their concerns with reality show about moonshiners and pawn brokers, have become the people who decide the direction of the United States. They are, after all, the ones who fight the wars. They don't have the luxury of a deferment for bone spurs.

The uneducated 'basket of deplorables' as Hillary Clinton labelled them, are almost the only people who bothered to vote in 2016. Their sentiment was cultivated by the thin disdain of the media, the unbridled avarice and greed of politicians, and their own pathetic prejudices fueled by a system that most certainly has left them far, far behind.

The Gadsden flag is a variation of a theme that was put forth by Benjamin Franklin in his newspaper in 1751. His newspaper, the Pennsylvania Gazettes, carried a bitter editorial protesting the British practice of sending convicts to America. The author suggested that the colonists return the favor by shipping "a cargo of rattlesnakes, which could be distributed in St. James Park, Spring Garden, and other places of pleasure, and particularly in the noblemen's gardens."

In 1754, Franklin printed a print of a snake as a commentary on the Albany Congress. To remind the delegates of the danger of disunity, the serpent was shown cut to pieces. Each segment is marked with the name of a colony, and the motto "Join or Die" below. Other newspapers took up the snake theme.

By 1774 the segments of the snake had grown together, and the motto had been changed to read: "United Now Alive and Free Firm on this Basis Liberty Shall Stand and Thus Supported Ever Bless Our Land Till Time Becomes Eternity"

I often wonder if my great-grandfather, Benjamin Andrew, was able to save his Gadsden flag when the British burned his house to the ground. He withstood the challenge and went on to become a legislator, President of Sam Houston's Council of Safety, and a hero of the American Revolution. I think of the agricultural innovations that Bartram mentions in his book, the 'seat of hospitality' that my great-grandfather and mother carved out for themselves there on Colonel's Island, the hope and promise they must have felt for a new world.

I think of him standing there, in that pleasant place, and watching it all burn to the ground.

Don't tread on me.

It's time to learn what that really means.

CHAPTER 10—GAMES OF CHANCE

So who are we, as Americans? To see the patriotic memes that flood the internet on national holidays—Independence Day, Memorial Day, Veteran's Day—you would think we are all in agreement. In that alternate reality of the sound byte and the meme, we love the flag. We love the concepts of freedom. We are brave. We are willing to fight injustice and oppression throughout the world, the real time equivalents of the Marvel Comics League of Justice. Our Marines are our superheroes. We cry when we see the flag, we cheer when we see our troops, we love the concepts of liberty. We are certain that we are living in the greatest country on earth, with the best people, the most resolve, the most resources, the strongest Constitution, and all the rest.

But what if that were just a lie? What if underneath all that political bluster, all the huff and blow of parades and whistle stops of political candidates, all the starry eyed wives of the modern defenders of liberty, we understood very little of what our culture actually stands for?

What if we have conveniently constructed an alternate reality, a media reality, one fueled by video games and movies and snippets of online conversations, one mile wide and one inch thick? What if we actually understand very little of true heroism, true sacrifice, truth liberty? And what if that lack of understanding is proving to be our undoing?

Just as we do poorly in understanding our geography, Americans are woefully weak when it comes to understanding the tenants of the government of the United States and how the Constitution, the Bill of Rights, and the three branches of government protect civil liberties.

According to the Annenberg Annual Civics Survey, nearly half of those surveyed (48 percent) say that freedom of speech is a right guaranteed by the First Amendment. But, unprompted, 37 percent could not name any First Amendment rights. And far fewer people could name the other First Amendment rights: 15 percent of respondents say freedom of religion; 14 percent say freedom of the press; 10 percent say the right of assembly; and only 3 percent say the right to petition the government.

The First Amendment reads:

Congress shall make no law respecting an establishment of religion, or prohibiting the free exercise thereof; or abridging the freedom of speech, or of the press; or the right of the people peaceably to assemble, and to petition the Government for a redress of grievances.

Contrary to the First Amendment, 39 percent of Americans support allowing Congress to stop the news media from reporting on any issue of national security without government approval. That was essentially unchanged from last year. But the survey, which followed a year of attacks on the news media, found less opposition to prior restraint (49 percent) than in 2016 (55 percent).

More than anything, Donald Trump is the image president. His largely uneducated voter base is more interested in the flag, the sound byte, the look of things than they are the messy reality of facts, the government, and the rule of law.

At the dawn of the age of television, social scientist Marshall McLuhan talked extensively about what he called the 'electronic fireside,' where families would collect around the television in much the same way that they collected around the radio to hear Roosevelt's fireside chats during the Great Depression.

In many ways, the media have become the makers of culture in modern America, replacing more traditional cultural sources such as families, communities, and education with a mass produced and stylized version of 'life in America.' "Just remember," says a popular meme, "when you're having a hard day, there is still some guy from your hometown who is trying to become a rapper."

In the past, the media's influence upon cultural groups was subjugated to community and cultural groups---we learned who we were, our role in society, and adopted cultural norms based upon people that we actually knew.

The increasing dependence upon the media for a shared knowledge base has two startling effects: first, knowledge groups increasingly depend upon the media for their cultural identity and, second, as time with the traditional groups dwindles, people willingly take the definitions offered by the media as a replacement for what they would otherwise know.

According to the members of the Cultural Indicators Research Team at the University of Pennsylvania's Annenberg School of Communications,

Television cultivates from the outset the very predispositions that affect cultural selections and uses. Transcending historic barriers of literacy and mobility, television has become the primary sourceof everyday culture in an otherwise heterogeneous population. Many of those now dependent upon television have never before been part of a shared national political culture.

The Annenberg team made this observation in the late 1980s. Here, in the age of Twitter and a 'tweeting president,' a shared cultural experience is shaped in real time by social media and reinforced by the 'buy in' from the recipients, often at the expense of common sense or as a result of weak common experiences and factual knowledge obtained from other, more traditional sources such as education or family values.

The brilliance (if we can call it that) of Trump's snake oil development of Make America Great Again is fully dependent upon his voter base cultivating their sense of reality based upon the images, ideas, statements, Tweets, and behaviors of the commander in chief. This is why he spends a disproportionate amount of time working on his base and his command over public opinion—rallies with cheering masses approving his unscripted riffs on everything from the work of journalists to foreign policy; midnight Tweets attacking everyone from Anthony Fauci to Rosie O'Donnell; his aggressive, seemingly uncaring remarks in times of crisis. His choices are not random, they are designed to help his base develop their own sense of culture, a culture that revolves around a reality that he and his cadre of sickeningly loyal conservative pundits relentlessly push to solidify their agenda and, thus, their power.

There's a lot of talk about what the President doesn't say in times of crisis. He didn't visit hurricane ravaged Puerto Rico until it became politically problematic to remain quiet, then he balanced that visit with infamously tossing rolls of paper towels to the suffering masses waiting to see him. He's obsessed with building a wall to further secure the United States border with Mexico, waxing poetic at every turn about how it will be a beautiful wall, a perfect wall, the most secure wall ever seen, a wall that Mexico will pay for, and on and on. He augments his agenda with the imagery more suited to a first rate propagandist such as Goebbels. "Bad guys" are swarming across the border. "Thugs with guns" are commandeering the streets. The global Muslim cabal, led by none other than Barack Obama if you believe Trump's hype, is threatening to destroy our way of life.

In every lie there is a wee bit of truth. And nobody does this better than Trump. He will take a factual event (the recent killing of George Floyd at the hands of the police in Minneapolis, for example) and then take it off in a fanciful direction with unfounded speculation.

As any student of old Perry Mason episodes will tell you, this is a standard tactic used to spread falsehoods and shore up an opinion base at the expense of the facts. Once the speculation is out there (the Democrats are coming for your guns. The rioters in the streets are

ANTIFA. COVID-19 was started in a Chinese lab and is a Democratic plot to disrupt the election) you can't take it back. And, in fact, Trump doesn't want to take it back. He's building a culture of believers, after all. Believers who don't know the facts. Believers who don't care about their own reality, who have built their concepts of the world not on history or education or science or even the things they might have learned at Granddad's knee, and supplanted them with the flimsy authority of media pundits and a president whose own sense of history and reverence for the truth is as hollow as a Hollywood soundstage.

Somewhere along the way we have lost the basic, fundamental elements upon which the United States was founded, replacing them with the folkloric stories of George Washington and the cherry tree, Thomas Jefferson writing the Constitution by candlelight, the woodsy ruggedness of Teddy Roosevelt, the ebonized nobility of Martin Luther King, Jr., the tough-talking cowboy rhetoric of Ronald Reagan, Camelot, the Star Spangled Banner.

Our concepts of nobility and heroism are skewed in favor of the stereotypical hero. After all, history is not necessarily sexy. Teachers grapple long and hard, every day, trying to make it appealing to students at all levels. In some states, social studies and civics have disappeared entirely. In others, the concepts of history education have nothing to do with taking field trips (states don't have the money for that) and first-hand accounts (again, money and time, who has time to listen to a Holocaust survivor or a veteran when testing is breathing down your neck like a relentless, multiple choice fire breathing dragon) for fiction. We are not talking. We are not listening.

It is the concept that has supplanted the prevalence of facts, of libraries, the importance of schools, the relevance of social studies, and the paramount understanding of where we come from with a weak, stylized version of the people who came before us and what they did for this country and the world.

Not everyone builds their understanding of a culture upon the media and, even among media consumers, there are those whose concepts are built otherwise. It is the failure of families and communities, coupled with an increasingly remote education system that values high stakes testing over the acquisition and application of factual knowledge. It is our disdain and disinterest in veterans and their stories, which matter little to us apart from those three times a year when we look up from our beer and hamburgers to supposedly pledge our undying gratitude for the 'ultimate sacrifice.'

If we really cared about our history and the American way of life, museums would not be grappling to stay afloat. Schools would not be struggling to host one veteran or one special event a year that might give students a firsthand, interactive experience—not an augmented, virtual reality experience, but actually sitting in a room and asking questions—with a person whose experience shaped history.

As I write this, here a few weeks after the killing of George Floyd, the American society is ablaze with rhetoric and symbolism. The statues of Confederate generals are being toppled to the ground. HBO just removed the Academy Award winning film, "Gone with the wind," from its catalogue of offerings because of the racist images presented. People are marching in the streets. Black Lives Matter is trending throughout the world.

This is needed. However, it has also been happening since the time of Dr. King. And, sadly, nothing has changed for the disenfranchised groups among us, the ones who have had to craft a culture developed solely on media images, not the reality of their experiences. The one whose stories remain to be told.

In failing to recognize the unvarnished truth of all of the people of our country, we are doomed to continue to live in communities that do not value diversity. We are doomed to develop the wrong notions that only a privileged few of us have access to, those of us who are already blessed with strong families and an understanding of where we came from, those of us whose lives have been bolstered by good teachers who cared about the world more than they cared about a test, by community leaders who knew us and understood the importance of every single person in a society, apart from the money they could make and the relentless march of the corruption of our leaders, the dereliction of our communities, and the callous, irrelevant messages of consumerism and false pride that swirl around us.

What has not been happening is a concerted, community effort to teach citizens about their own history, give them a stronger sense of their own place in America, and encourage them to fully understand the rights and responsibilities of being a citizen of the greatest country on earth.

My father's family has lived in a small corner of western North Carolina, known as Old Rutherford County, since before the

Revolutionary War. One of our great-grandfathers was Robert Morris, known as George Washington's War Hawk, the financier of the American Revolution. One of his relatives, Uncle Billy Morris, kept a fire going in a fireplace in Saluda, North Carolina for 164 years. It was known as the "Old Fire in the World." For 164 years four generations of the Morris family kept a fire going in the Holbert Cove area near Saluda that has been called "the oldest fire in the world."

Billy Morris, who died in 1944 at the age of 84, spent his life keeping the fire going.

The original "chunk of wood" was laid in 1780, Morris told writers in the 1930s and '40s.

The Morris fire became so famous that Billy was asked to appear on a national radio show out of New York City and his story was written in newspapers across the country.
Ed Leland of Saluda took Morris to New York City in 1937 for the radio show.

"He talked a few minutes and played a fiddle on the radio," Leland said.

On that show Morris said, "I live alone in a little log cabin back in the hills of Saluda, N.C. I've got a little piece of ground, a cow, four pigs and a horse.

"   The fire has to be handled with real skill and care. I cover it with ashes and during the day there's a softly glowing brand resting on a bed of red hot ashes, and it doesn't give off a bit of smoke.

"After the chores are done at night, I come and stir up the fire 'til it's a blazing, and then I sit down before it … and I can see in the flames my mother and father, my grandparents and my great-grandparents who started it burning. Sometimes I sit with my old fiddle and play to it."

Then Morris played "Bonaparte's Retreat" to a national listening audience.

Our society is failing because we fail to value the history, the stories, the significance of the people in our own communities. We care more about the Kardashians than we do about the elderly woman living in the house at the end of our street. We don't know where we came from, we don't know the sacrifices that people made to get us to this modern time, we don't care about the contributions of all people, valuing some lives more than others and ignored the educational systems, cultural mores, and messages that would revere all those around us. We make efforts to celebrate and understand the culture of the white patriarchy at the expense of everyone else. What we should be doing is helping each person discover their inner truth, where they came from, their inner ethics, the nobility that is in all of us.

We allow people like Donald Trump and his myopic, malevolent worldview take precedence over our own heritage, the things we know to be true, and give credence to the experiences of a few rather than the importance of every single person in the country. Each person has a story that is vital to the making of America. Each person's experience is needed, is required, if we are to succeed as a nation. The disenfranchised among us should not have to march in the streets and topple statues to assert their rights under the law or expect that the country that is their home should be a refuge for their families, their culture, and their way of life.

The media are complicit in the dusty erosion of American ethics and the rule of law. They favor short snippets of information over the long form narrative and ensuing context that people really need to understand what's happening around them. As a person who grew up in rural North Carolina, I know how 'my people' are stereotyped and depicted in the popular press. Our cultural icons are seen as stupid, weak, backwards, uneducated, and prejudiced. We are seen either as the crazy hillbillies of Deliverance, the redneck swirling of Bo Duke, or the animal loving sexpots such as Ellie May Clampett. We are not seen as engineers. Our people of color are not recognized. The only story I can think of about life in North Carolina had to do with a man who had a coon dog that could climb a tree, a man who eventually made his way to Johnny Carson's show.

I am an educated person with only the vaguest of southern drawls. Invariably, when I an interviewing someone, they ask where I am from and express nothing short of amazement when I tell them I was born in a small town in western North Carolina. But you didn't grow up there, they press. Actually, yes I did. Why is it so impossible to believe that a person whose roots have been in the mountains of North Carolina could also be articulate and educated, well travelled, not prejudiced, a person whose ancestors could quote Shakespeare and financed the American revolution.

As consumers, we should choose context over memes and the long view over games. We can no longer afford to allow the media to shape our cultural morals the expense of the people around us..

t's telling that in a country that pays lip service to Veterans, led by a president whose press secretary and advisors insist publicly "loves this country," more than anything. There are more than 70,000 homeless veterans in the United States.

We should expect that a president tell us the truth. Not try to influence our own thinking at the expense of our dignity.

We should learn to listen to the stories of the people around us. Believe them to be true. Help those who have no knowledge of their place in the world to find it, to know their worth apart from the fuzzy lenses of propagandistic drivel that insists that some people are more valuable than others. We should build schools that teach children the value of their history and celebrates the cultures of all of us, not just the white and privileged and the ones who had access to good parents and clean communities. We all deserve that.

Our society can no longer depend upon the media for their structure. We can no longer assume that schools are doing a good job and speak for all of us. We must change the dialogue to one that helps each individual find their individual worth. We need a president who leads, not one that spends every waking moment using the gaps in the knowledge of the people around him to manipulate and diminish their world view.

CHAPTER 11—HALL OF MIRRORS

Travelling carnivals were the highlight of community life for poor children in 1930s and 40s America. Rural schoolchildren would save their money and, when the carnival pulled in and set up in a dirt field just out of town, they were ready for the dubious delights that would await. The two headed man! The house of mirrors! Games of chance.

The success of any con game depends somewhat on distraction and somewhat on the gullibility of the subject. At the old time carnivals, the games of chance were rigged against you. The sweet treats were sweet only for a moment, cotton candy that lasts for a second on the tongue before it evaporates. As for the dangerous monkeys, the extent of their terror depended upon what you didn't know about monkeys in the first place.

Donald Trump's foreign policy is much like the carnival that pulls into town, dependent upon the short view of a subset of the American people for its success. If you are a student of history, if you understand the role that the long game plays in geopolitics, if you know the geographic hot spots of the world and can identify their meaning to the United States both politically and economically, you are far less dazzled by the shell game perpetrated by Trump and his aggressive, belligerent, propagandistic gang of cronies.

In the mid-2000s, my husband and I travelled 3,000 miles along the Silk Route of Pakistan from Karachi high into the Himalayan mountains. At one point, we still on a small platform in the little village of Jaglote. There, in the distance, is the juncture of the three greatest mountain ranges in the world: the Himalaya, the Karakoram, and the HinduKush.

The Silk Route is a road of conquerors and legends. It is of great geopolitical significance, as Pakistan and India skirmish over the control of Kashmir and China makes inroads that will establish a warm-water port in the Pakistani seaport of Gwadar, a short for Chinese trade that will circumvent the Russians. The United States brought engineers to the area in the mid-50s to survey the economic potential and decided to leave well enough alone. The modern Chinese, with their interest in global trade domination, did not see it that way and have invested millions in what will be one of the most pivotal deep sea ports in the world.

The stereotypical, isolationistic world view is myopic and ultimately destructive to the best interests of the American people. It is a fiction, built on the fantasies of wild west movies and the dubious mythology of personal independence and the feeling that we have everything we need without the influence of the world.

The uneducated among Trump's voter base, the ones who cannot name the capitals of the states in the United States, much less identify the members of the United Nations Security Council, love this sort of fiery rhetoric at the expense of facts. The 'big stick' approach appeals to their sense of vanity and the stereotypical symbols of patriotism that pay nothing more than lip service to the notion of American ideals; it's an approach that is far from the considered, research based, long game of foreign policy that actually has a chance of accomplishing the ideals we supposedly covet as Americans—the rule of law, a clean environment, a better life for the citizens around the world.

Trump has made the long game all about economics and the bottom line. Who cares if the people of Syria, so desperate to leave, risk everything? Who cares if innocent children die in bombings in Afghanistan or if thousands of children in sub-Saharan Africa die as a result of disease and a lack of clean drinking water.

Former UN Ambassador Nikki Haley visited the UN Headquarters in New York in 2017, delivering a fiery rhetorical speech that talked a lot about America "getting its money's worth," one of the key talking points of the Trump Administration.
She said,

At the UN, we're constantly asked to do more and give more -- in the past we have. So, when we make a decision, at the will of the American people, about where to locate OUR embassy, we don't expect those we've helped to target us," Haley wrote on Facebook and Twitter on Tuesday evening. "On Thursday, there will be a vote at the UN criticizing our choice. And yes, the US will be taking names.

Taking names is more of the province of 6th grade narcs than it is the leader of the free world. And yet, here we are, pitted against almost every nation in the world, dropping out of the World Health Organization as a global pandemic has killed more than 170,000 Americans and infected millions throughout the world. At a moment when the concepts of global cooperation actually affect the well-being of American families and the lives of millions, Trump's tunnel vision focuses not on the good that can be done and the ways in which we can alleviate the suffering from COVID-19, but the almighty dollar that could possibly be made.

At a press conference touting supposed positive job growth, just a few weeks after the murder of George Floyd at the hands of a police officer, Trump even invoked the spirit of the murder victim, surmising that even George (who, let us be clear, had been murdered and was cold in the ground, hardly the place to enjoy the benefits of a growing economy) would appreciate the positive numbers.

In White House remarks that folded digressions within digressions, Trump declared: "Today is probably, if you think of it, the greatest comeback in American history."
Speaking after the 10th night of mass anti-racism protests across the country, Trump suggested that Floyd, who died after a white Minneapolis police officer pressed his knee on his neck for nearly nine minutes, would be happy about the figures.

Hopefully George is looking down right now and saying this a great thing that's happening for our country," he said. "There's a great day for him. It's a great day for everybody. It's a great day for everybody. There's a great, great day in terms of equality.

No, Ringmaster Don, it's not a great day for everybody. A great day for everybody is when no one of any color is bullied or dies at the hands of a corrupt system. George is not looking down like some sort of ebonized angel, smiling on the country that he left behind when his head was crammed underneath a patrol car and a corrupt police officer held his knee on his neck until he drew his last breath. A great day would be when people are listened to and have meaning work. When children can play in safety without needless gun violence. When people don't worry about where their next meal will come from or how they will pay for their medicine this month. There are no ethnic angels hovering above, the sweet departed souls of the members of the Mother Emmanuel Church, for instance, guiding the good people of America in the happy construction of well-baked pound cakes or nicely mown grass.

This comment, like almost every comment out of this snake oil huckster's mouth, is making an idiot of you, just in the same way that the carnival barkers at the old time country fair had you convinced that ghosts would jump out of mirrors or that you could really win a teddy bear by paying close attention to a game of chance.

This country, based on hopes and dreams, needs more than wishes to make a fair society a reality. It needs an educated electorate, a group of voters who consider their lives in this country a privilege and voting a duty. It takes schools that abandon nonsensical testing and parental pressure for the good work that the teachers of this country could do if they had the resources from the federal government to educate all children. It takes people who can find China on a map and don't buy in to whimsical conspiracy theories that a global pandemic that has killed millions is a hoax or the vague, benign notion that the opposing political party is 'coming for your guns' and 'want to keep you from gathering in church' despite their own best advice.

Here are the signs I believe in:

- It's a bad sign when the voter turnout in the last election was roughly half of the eligible voters managed to vote.

- It's a bad sign when of those who did vote for the sitting president, 30% of them did not have a basic, high school education.

- It's a bad sign when a sitting president, rather than understanding the systemic racism and pandemic pain experienced by historically disenfranchised groups, chooses to make a cartoonish martyr out of a dead black man and attempt to use that symbol to tout his own horn, prematurely and without reason, to feather his own nest.

- It's a bad sign when Daddy's Little Girl becomes a presidential advisor while key policy advisors, retired five star generals, and qualified people are let go as a result of a presidential tantrum.

As a media person, I don't want a media celebrity as the President of the United States. I don't need to be entertained by a squinty eyed, puffy leader with a lumbering gait, a bad spray tan, and a bizarre yellow hairpiece. I'd like to have someone who understands the gravitas of the position.

"Congratulations," said comedian Dave Chappell in his Saturday Night Monologue a few days before Trump's inauguration in 2017, "you've elected the first internet troll as your president."

I have voted in every election for which I was qualified to vote since I was old enough to vote. In my family, my father would get the sample ballot out of the local newspaper and we would, in the ensuing weeks, research the candidates and their issues. We would then take our sample with us on election day to make sure we had voted in the manner that aligned with our values. We'd vote if it was raining. We would vote if we were sick. If it was freezing cold. It was our duty. It was our right. It was the privilege that our ancestors fought for when they left England in the 1600s and made a new life in America.

They died on the battlefields at Kings Mountain, North Carolina. They died on the battlefield at Gaines Mill, Virginia. They died on the battlefields in Verdun, France. They died in St. Lo, France. They died in Vietnam.

They did not die so that less than 60% of the qualified voters, themselves uneducated, could pick a guy who had an entertaining television show as the leader of the free world and subsequently run it into the ground.

There are moments when one thinks that nothing can be done to save our society. In my heart, I do not believe this to be true. I am the child of teachers and scientists and politicians and patriots and also of slave traders and plantation owners and war hawks and senators. They crossed oceans and fought battles for the cause of liberty. It was not something that came without personal cost, nor was it embarked upon without a personal, theoretical structure behind it that went far beyond anything one hears about in academic books.

It is difficult to watch the news, here in the summer of 2020, with anything other than the mantle of absolute dread. People are dying in the streets. People are dying alone. The President and his cronies head for their underground bunker with a seemingly amazing disregard for the people around them. The entire world seems as if it might go up into flames.

Ultimately, the answer lies in our ability to reinvent ourselves, on the personal level. We must understand who we are, where we come from as a people, who we are personally. We must realize what it means to be an individual and help those who have been disenfranchised, the subjects of centuries of systemic abuse—ethnic, economic, social, political—and decide, on a personal level, that we are no longer going to tolerate that abuse. We must help every person to find their own individual worth and honor that. We must target corruption and eliminate it.

We can no longer afford to live in a house of mirrors. The answer starts with us—our families, our understanding of the world, our honor and values, our reverence for the Constitution and its meaning, not empty symbols. We have to want all of those around us to enjoy life in the manner that we would want for ourselves. We have to make amends.

Lynn Morris is a writer and journalist specializing in the role of the media and stereotyping. A graduate of the University of South Carolina's Graduate School of Journalism and Mass Communications, she has spoken about media, power, and politics at the United Nations in New York, at universities throughout Europe, and in South Asia. Her writing for the popular news media about luxury travel and architecture has been featured in magazines including Bon Appetit, Cigar Aficionado, Town & Country, Robb Report, Polo Magazine, Veranda, and Outside. She lives and writes at Stargrove, a 200 acre organic farm in the mountains of western North Carolina, which she shares with her husband, who is a former member of the famed cavalry regiment, King Edward V's Own Lancers, the Bengal Lancers.

She is currently at work on a book about her road trek through the Himalayan mountains of Pakistan along the famed Silk Road.